WORDS OF WISDOM FROM
FAMOUS MEXICAN AMERICANS

"To have this job you must enjoy the work because you will do lots of it! You must be available to others and sacrifice your own wishes. You must be patient to strike a compromise. You must be directed to work. But you don't mind because you are fulfilled and productive!" —Henry Cisneros

"What I like most about my job is to be able to change things for people, to change things for the better. We must use our lives to make the world a better place, not just to acquire things. That is what we are put on earth for."
—Dolores Huerta

"I am eager to learn from others. My father believed you could learn from 'Un peon o un presidente'—a farm worker or a president—and you should respect both equally."
—Blandina Cardenas Ramirez

"Real success in life is knowing that you helped others to change their lives for the better." —Dan Sosa, Jr.

"Whenever you run into an obstacle there is a creative way around it. Remember, your greatest strength and powers and treasures are within you, and you carry around all you need to deal with your own life." —Luis Valdez

D0770014

OTHER PUFFIN BOOKS YOU MAY ENJOY

City Within a City: How Kids Live in New York's Chinatown
Kathleen Krull

The Other Side: How Kids Live in a California Latino Neighborhood
Kathleen Krull

Pueblo Boy: Growing Up in Two Worlds
Marcia Keegan

FAMOUS
MEXICAN
AMERICANS

Janet Morey &
Wendy Dunn

ILLUSTRATED WITH PHOTOGRAPHS

PUFFIN BOOKS

Some of the photographs in this book are treasured family pictures. All are used by permission and through the courtesy of the following: Victor Aleman, United Farm Workers, 8, 12; The Archives of Labor and Urban Affairs, Wayne State University, 11; The Artists Agency, 95; Mr. and Mrs. J. George Cisneros (parents), 17, 18; Archbishop Patrick Flores, 30, 34, 36, 37; *Golf World*, 59; Nancy Lopez, 55, 61; MALDEF Archives, 69; Luis Nogales, 77, 79, 86; Pedro Olmos, 90, 94; Bob Poston, 50; Blandina Cardenas Ramirez, 109, 110, 113; Edward Roybal, 125, 127; Norm Schindler/ASUCLA, 72; Justice Dan Sosa, Jr., 131, 135, 137; SVREP, San Antonio, Texas, 162, 164; Office of the Treasury, 102; Luis Valdez, 142, 144, 151; Mary Louise Velasquez, 155, 157; © Oscar Williams 1986, 24; Lori Ybarra, 40, 43.

PUFFIN BOOKS
Published by the Penguin Group
Penguin Books USA Inc., 375 Hudson Street, New York, New York 10014, U.S.A.
Penguin Books Ltd, 27 Wrights Lane, London W8 5TZ, England
Penguin Books Australia Ltd, Ringwood, Victoria, Australia
Penguin Books Canada Ltd, 10 Alcorn Avenue, Toronto, Ontario, Canada M4V 3B2
Penguin Books (N.Z.) Ltd, 182-190 Wairau Road, Auckland 10, New Zealand

Penguin Books Ltd, Registered Offices: Harmondsworth, Middlesex, England

First published in the United States of America by Cobblehill Books,
an affiliate of Dutton Children's Books,
a division of Penguin Books USA Inc., 1989
Published in Puffin Books, 1997

10 9 8 7 6 5 4 3 2 1

THE LIBRARY OF CONGRESS HAS CATALOGED THE COBBLEHILL EDITION AS FOLLOWS:
Morey, Janet.
Famous Mexican Americans / Janet Morey & Wendy Dunn.
p. cm. Bibliography: p. Includes index.
Summary: Discusses the accomplishments and contributions to society of fourteen Mexican Americans, representing a variety of professions.
ISBN 0-525-65012-1
1. Mexican Americans—Biography—Juvenile literature.
[1. Mexican Americans—Biography.] I. Dunn, Wendy. II. Title.
E184.M5M67 1989 920'.00926872073—dc20 [B]
[920] 89-7218 CIP AC

Puffin Books ISBN 0-14-038437-5
Printed in the United States of America

Acknowledgments

We would like to thank our editor, Joe Ann Daly, for suggesting that we write this book, and for providing continual assistance throughout the project. We are also grateful to Dr. Luis Leal for writing the splendid, comprehensive Foreword.

We greatly appreciate the interviews and assistance granted by the following participants in this volume: Henry Cisneros, Dolores Huerta, Nancy Lopez, Vilma Martinez, Luis Nogales, Blandina Cardenas Ramirez, Edward Roybal, Dan Sosa, Jr., Luis Valdez, and Willie Velasquez.

We also thank the following: Cesar Chavez and Marc Grossman, a former longtime aide; Marshelle Valila of the United Farm Workers; Mrs. Elvira Cisneros, the mayor's mother; Office of the Mayor, San Antonio, Texas; Archbishop Patrick Flores and his secretary, Myrtle G. Sanchez; Lori Ybarra, Alicia

Huerta Hernandez, and Vincent Huerta, three of
Dolores Huerta's children; Mary L. Wenzel of the
International Management Group, and Julie Gumlia
and Sandi Owen of the Ladies Professional Golf
Association, who assisted with Nancy Lopez's chap-
ter; the Mexican American Legal Defense and Ed-
ucational Fund; Edward James Olmos; Pedro
Olmos, father of Edward Olmos; Daniel A. Haro,
associate of Edward Olmos, and Jules, The Artists
Agency; Katherine Davalos Ortega and June Gayle
Turner at the United States Treasury; Mrs. Amelia
B. Cardenas, mother of Blandina Cardenas Ramirez,
and Nancy R. Lopez, assistant to Dr. Ramirez; Assemblywoman Lucille Roybal Allard, daughter of
Congressman Roybal, and his staff assistants in the
Los Angeles and Washington, D.C., offices; Michael
Stipanich of the Writers & Artists Agency, who
helped with Luis Valdez's chapter; Gladys Alonzo
at the Southwest Voter Registration Education Pro-
ject; Jane Sarabia Velasquez, widow of Willie Ve-
lasquez; Mary Louise Velasquez, his mother; and
Richard Chabran, librarian at the Chicano Studies
Research Center at UCLA.

Special thanks to members of our families, Jack
Morey, Bruce Dunn, and Julie Dunn; Allen Michel,
our legal advisor; and Lloyd Kajikawa, who offered
computer assistance.

Preface

★ *A famous movie writer-director began his
   career in the fields of California*
★ *Full of self-confidence, a young girl overcame
   discrimination and discouragement to later
   become a leading attorney*
★ *A young mother wanted to help farm workers
   and became that union's vice president*

There is a story behind every successful person.
These are just glimpses of three of the fourteen famous Mexican Americans presented in this book. All
share a common heritage and have made important
contributions to our society, while they represent a
variety of professions and accomplishments.

Each life story traces the roots of achievement.
Most of these fourteen prominent people were personally interviewed for this project. They provided

childhood memories, current information, and special insights. Often, their family members furnished further background and treasured photographs. In the cases of those too busy for a personal interview, top aides and assistants supplied information. All subjects have approved the material about themselves.

The occupations and importance of these outstanding individuals are explained, as well as related institutions within which they have worked, such as the Mexican American Legal Defense and Educational Fund (MALDEF), the Southwest Voter Registration Education Project (SVREP), the U.S. Commission on Civil Rights.

Information about many of these individuals is drawn from adult-level sources. This volume will introduce some very significant Mexican Americans, and provides updated material on some others with whom young readers may be more familiar.

Foreword

The United States of America is a country made up of people whose ancestors, in early years, came here mostly from Europe; others were brought here from Africa, and a lesser number came from Asia and other parts of the world. All these people brought with them their own cultures and ethnic backgrounds, not two of which were alike. Among them, however, those who spoke English prevailed.

Before 1848 there were hardly any Spanish-speaking people in what was then the United States. That year, however, something happened that changed not only the geographical nature of the nation, but also its ethnic composition as well as its history.

During the 1830s that nation had begun to expand to the south and the west in order to fulfill what was then called its "manifest destiny." People from the southern states went to Texas, which in 1836, due to their influence, decided to declare its independence from Mexico. Mexico agreed to give this large territory its freedom, provided it would not join the Union as a state. When the Republic of Texas requested statehood, and was admitted in 1845, the result led to the U.S.-Mexican War, which was declared by the United States in 1846 and lasted until 1848. During the spring of that year Mexico signed the Treaty of Guadalupe Hidalgo, by means of which what is now called the Southwest was ceded to the United States.

According to the Treaty, the Mexican people living in the ceded territories could go back to Mexico or remain in the Southwest and become American citizens. Most of them decided to stay, since their ancestors had lived there for generations. They became the oldest ethnic group of the nation, the frontiers of which now extended from the Atlantic to the Pacific and south to the Rio Grande River, the new southern border.

What were the cultural and ethnic features that distinguished this new group of citizens of the United States? The ancient Aztec Empire in central Mexico and that of the Mayas of Yucatan in the south, with their highly developed cultures, ended— the Aztecs in 1521 with the conquest of Tenochtitlán (Mexico City today) by Hernan Cortez and his Spanish conquistadores, and the Mayas in 1546. The predominance of the native populations ended, but not the influence of their cultures or the presence of their blood in their descendants.

The Spaniards who conquered Mexico were not only looking for gold. From the ancient Aztec capital they set out to look for Utopia. Some went south to El Dorado; others to Florida to look for the fountain of youth; and some to the north, to the land known to the Aztecs as Aztlán (their original home), to the land of the Seven Cities of Cibola, Quivira, and California. These lands later came to be known as Texas, Arizona, New Mexico, Colorado, and California.

Although the number of Mexican people living in the Southwest was not large, it was gradually increased by the arrival of new immigrants from Mexico. The reasons for their coming here were many, the most important being the lack of steady employment in Mexico, political turmoil there, and the economic expansion of the Southwest due to the industrial and agricultural revolutions. Workers were needed in the fields and in the factories. With the change from cattle raising to agriculture, more and more field hands were needed to work in the former pasturelands, now turned into rich producers of cotton, corn, fruits, and all types of produce with which to feed the nation. Large numbers of workers crossed the border to cultivate the fields of Texas, Arizona, and California.

Another factor affecting the increase of immigration to this country was the Mexican Revolution which took place between 1910 and 1920. The trend, however, was reversed during the '30s, due to the Great Depression when thousands of workers went back to Mexico. This period in the history of the Mexican Americans came to an end in 1941, when many of them joined the armed forces to fight in Europe and the Orient. In most recent years the economic crisis through which Mexico is passing has again driven many workers here in search of a better life. The passing of new immigration laws in 1987, however, has stopped this trend.

All these immigrants have brought with them Mexico's culture, with which they have enriched not only that of Mexican Americans, but also that of all Americans. The contributions of their descendants have been significant. In this book you will read about the accomplishments of some representative Mexican Americans who have been recognized for their outstanding contributions: Cesar Chavez in the field of labor relations; Henry Cisneros, Edward Roybal, and William Velasquez in the field of politics; Archbishop Patrick Flores in religious service; Luis Nogales in business; Edward James Olmos and Luis Valdez in the arts; and Dan Sosa, Jr., as a Senior Justice. During the '80s, Mexican-American women distinguished themselves in all fields. Their contributions have equaled, and sometimes surpassed, those of men. Here you will read about some of these prominent Mexican American women: Dolores Huerta,

Nancy Lopez, Vilma Martinez, Katherine Davalos Ortega, and Dr. Blandina Cardenas Ramirez. An encyclopedia would be needed to tell about the contributions of Mexican Americans to contemporary American life and culture. What you are about to read deals with the lives of some representative Mexican Americans who have distinguished themselves in their chosen fields and have been recognized by their fellow Americans for their contributions. It is hoped that their struggles, their unselfish and humanistic goals, in a word, their lives, may inspire you and others to carry on their excellent work. These Americans of Mexican descent have demonstrated that there are no limits to what a person can accomplish if inspired by faith in humanity and a desire to contribute to improve society, as the people about whom you are going to read have done, many of them at the cost of great sacrifice.

Dr. Luis Leal
Goleta, California

Dr. Luis Leal was born in Linares, Mexico. He received his Ph.D. in Spanish from the University of Chicago in 1950 and is Professor Emeritus of Latin American Literature at the University of Illinois, Champaign-Urbana. Currently he is Visiting Professor, Department of Chicano Studies, University of California, Santa Barbara. He is the author of numerous books and articles on Latin American literature, especially Mexican and Chicano literature.

Contents

Foreword by Dr. Luis Leal   *ix*

CESAR CHAVEZ   1
   President, United Farm Workers

HENRY CISNEROS   14
   Mayor, San Antonio, Texas

PATRICK FLORES   27
   Archbishop, San Antonio, Texas

DOLORES HUERTA   39
   Vice President, United Farm Workers

NANCY LOPEZ   51
   Golfer

VILMA MARTINEZ   63
   Attorney

LUIS NOGALES   75
   Business Executive

EDWARD JAMES OLMOS   88
   Actor

KATHERINE DAVALOS ORTEGA   98
   Treasurer of the United States

BLANDINA CARDENAS RAMIREZ   106
   Member, U.S. Commission on Civil Rights

EDWARD R. ROYBAL   119
   United States Congressman

DAN SOSA, JR.   130
   Justice, New Mexico State Supreme Court

LUIS VALDEZ   140
   Writer / Film Director

WILLIAM VELASQUEZ   153
   Former President, Southwest Voter
   Registration Education Project

Selected Bibliography   167
Index   172

Cesar Chavez

Cesar Chavez risked his life during the summer of 1988. He did not eat for thirty-six days. He was fasting to protest the use of pesticides which he said were dangerous to consumers, farm workers, and to the environment. The sixty-one-year-old Chavez grew weaker every day, but his action attracted attention and support for his cause. When he finally broke his fast, it was Ethel Kennedy, widow of Senator Robert F. Kennedy, who handed him a small piece of bread. Others, including the Reverend Jesse Jackson and actors Martin Sheen, Robert Blake, and Edward James Olmos each vowed to carry on his protest by not eating for three days.

This was not the first time that Cesar Chavez had fasted to draw attention to an issue. It was not the first time that he suffered so that others might benefit. Much of his life has been devoted to helping migrant farm workers gain rights, and oftentimes that has meant personal sacrifice.

Cesar Chavez has been president of the United Farm Workers for over twenty-five years, representing farm workers in dealing with growers. Ironically, Mr. Chavez has said that he might have become a grower himself if his family had not lost their farm during the Depression of the 1930s. As things turned out, he came to know firsthand the way of life and the problems of the migrant workers.

Cesar's grandfather, Cesario, left Chihuahua, Mexico, during difficult political times in the 1880s. He came to the United States, found work, and when he had earned enough money, he sent for his family—his wife, Dorotea, and their fourteen children. The Chavezes homesteaded on over one hundred acres near Yuma, Arizona, in 1909, three years before Arizona was even a state. Cesario built a house of adobe with walls eighteen inches thick. By the time the house was finished, there was another child in the family.

Librado Chavez, one of the sons, was only two at the time he came to the United States. He worked with his father as he was growing up, and in 1924, he married Juana Estrada, who was also from Chihuahua. The following year he bought a business nearby which included a pool hall, a garage, and a grocery store where the family lived. On March 31,

1927, their second child, Cesar Estrada Chavez, was born in that grocery store.

When Cesar was very young, business was good for Librado Chavez. He was even made postmaster, since people had their mail delivered at his store. But then the Great Depression began. All across the country people lost their jobs, and businesses suffered. Librado Chavez was forced to sell and move back to the adobe house with his family. They were poor, but for a time they continued to farm and ranch, until the economic situation became worse. People had no money to buy what they needed. Sometimes they would barter with whatever they had. When Cesar's younger sister, Vicky, was born, the doctor was paid with watermelons. When the Chavezes were unable to pay the taxes, the family farm was sold at auction. The Chavez children watched as bulldozers uprooted their favorite trees.

Cesar's parents packed their Studebaker, became migrant workers in California, and began a more difficult life. Sometimes they were forced to live out of that car, at other times it was in tarpaper shacks or tents. Pay was low and the work was hard, often with long hours in the hot sun. As they followed the crops, Cesar attended over thirty schools, but found it difficult to keep up and dropped out of school by the eighth grade. The family was also exposed to more racism than they had experienced as landowners. They quickly realized that migrants had little control over their lives. They valued the freedom they had known, and felt that they and other workers should still be treated fairly even though they were migrants.

Cesar Chavez got an early lesson in farm labor unions when his father and uncle joined a succession of them. They supported workers who went on strike in an effort to get their employers to bargain with them. Cesar learned tactics and strategy, but none of these early farm unions was very successful or survived. Migrant workers were difficult to organize, since they moved so much as they followed the harvests, and their poverty meant that it was hard to get money to run a union.

Cesar was affected by his own work experiences, his father's involvement, and also by his mother's teachings. Juana Chavez was against fighting and violence. She insisted that her children learn to share, and to adopt a casual attitude toward money. These early influences have guided Cesar Chavez throughout his life.

When Cesar was fifteen, he met Helen Fabela in Delano, California. Helen's parents were originally from Mexico, but she had been born in Brawley, California. She worked in the fields, and also in a grocery store after school. When Cesar and Helen met, World War II had already begun. Their dating was interrupted when he enlisted in the Navy at seventeen and was sent to the Pacific. Back home after the war, Cesar resumed life as a farm worker, but he married Helen in 1948 and they honey-mooned for two weeks, touring old California missions by car.

Helen and Cesar Chavez settled in San Jose, where Cesar worked in a lumberyard. The *barrio* where they lived was called "Sal Si Puedes," which means "Get Out If You Can." This poor area attracted people studying urban problems, and it also drew people who wanted to help the residents directly. Father Donald McDonnell founded a small church in the *barrio* which helped people relate their religion to their daily difficulties. Fred Ross came to establish a chapter of the Community Service Organization (CSO), a group which encouraged residents to become involved in solving their own problems. Cesar Chavez learned from both these men.

At first, Chavez volunteered for the CSO, working with voter registration. In 1952, he took a full-time job with the CSO, and learned to use local "house meetings" to organize people and recruit volunteers. Later he used these techniques with farm workers. During this period, Cesar broadened his own education as he became more aware of politics and read biographies of labor leaders.

Many of the people in the CSO were farm workers, although the CSO did not deal with their labor problems. Cesar wanted to form an organization to help those farm workers. He could not convince the CSO to go in this direction, so he left his job with them and formed the National Farm Workers Association (NFWA), with many others who were willing to organize and sacrifice. These included Dolores Huerta, his cousin Manuel, and several ministers. Helen Chavez would also become an important part of the union. In eleven months Cesar Chavez visited eighty-seven communities and labor camps, and held many house meetings. An Aztec-style eagle was chosen as the union's emblem.

Meanwhile, Cesar and Helen's family had grown to eight children. Helen worked and raised them while her husband traveled often. But Cesar involved the youngsters when he could. His son Fernando remembers handing out leaflets during his childhood. Cesar had organized the union with $1,200 from his savings account, some of Helen's wages as a farm worker, and loans and gifts from relatives. However, he would not take money from another group similar to his, which wanted to help. He felt that the farm workers had to support and sacrifice for their own union. He himself took no pay and worked long hours. Workers would donate food and clothing. He wanted his union to involve its members, both in contributing money and making decisions. He also wanted all activities to be nonviolent. He is a very religious person, and greatly admired Mahatma Gandhi and Martin Luther King, Jr., leaders who were dedicated to nonviolence.

Cesar Chavez was well aware of the problems facing migrant farm workers—the poor working and living conditions, low wages and no benefits such as health insurance or a credit union from which they could borrow money. Many growers made their workers use a short-handled hoe, which forced them to stoop and created back problems. During World War II, the *bracero* program was started. Thousands of Mexican field hands were brought into the Southwest and particularly to California when the crops were ready to harvest, then trucked back to Mexico when the work was finished. They were given jobs instead of local workers. Additionally, farm workers were frequently discouraged from organizing to improve their situations. The National Farm Workers Association wanted a chance to represent the workers in dealing with the growers. Slowly, the union grew as it provided services and promised a better life.

Labor unions often use strikes, with employees refusing to work, to pressure employers into bargaining. But with farm labor, strikes were more difficult, since the growers were easily able to hire other workers. During the first strike against grape growers in 1965, Cesar Chavez realized that something more effective was needed, so a grape boycott was organized. During a boycott, people do not buy or use a product, and the producers of that product usually lose money and decide to change their ways. The grape boycott involved other unions, church groups, and consumers all over the country who refused to handle or buy grapes. Grape growers were pressured into bargaining and signing contracts with

the union. The boycott also increased public awareness and support for Mr. Chavez and his work, and it was a nonviolent means of protest. The union has sponsored similar boycotts through the years.

Cesar Chavez has used fasting as another nonviolent way of attracting attention to problems he wants solved. In 1968, he fasted for twenty-five days during the grape boycott. He had Senator Robert Kennedy's support. Just months before Senator Kennedy was killed by an assassin's bullet, he handed Cesar the piece of bread that ended that fast. Mr. Chavez also fasted again in 1972 and 1988.

By 1972, the NFWA had merged with another group and became a member of the AFL-CIO, a large organization composed of many labor unions. The United Farm Workers of America (UFW) became the new name for Cesar Chavez's union. Initially, the union had worked out of Delano, but in the early 1970s, the Chavez family, along with the union, moved their headquarters to La Paz on land purchased by a supporter and donated to the union. It was the site of a former tuberculosis sanitorium, southeast of Delano.

The UFW has had victories and setbacks. It has provided benefits such as a medical plan, an educa-

Cesar Chavez (left front, with sunglasses) leading farm workers on a march in San Francisco during the grape boycott, 1984.

tion fund, pension money for retirement. There are better working conditions, and procedures for workers to voice complaints. The *bracero* program ended, but imported foreign workers are still a problem. In 1975, the short-handled hoe was outlawed, but later was reconsidered. Also in 1975, a state board concerned with labor relations between farm workers, and growers was established in California. However, the union believes that the board's effectiveness has decreased, and the numbers of UFW members and contracts with growers have declined. Recently, though, there has been an emphasis by the UFW to increase public involvement and awareness, using advanced technology which reaches supporters all over the country. *The Wrath of Grapes*, a video that discusses some pesticides and their effects, is being distributed to interested groups and shown in some schools. Computerized mailings are sent out.

UFW headquarters at La Paz reflect the progress made by the union. There is a library, a chapel, a meeting hall, and buildings housing the pension program and credit union, run by Helen Chavez. There is a computer and printing center where son Paul works with graphics and direct mailings. There are homes for about two hundred union leaders and staff volunteers.

Cesar and Helen Chavez live in a small wood-frame house in La Paz. The home and food are provided, but Cesar Chavez is the lowest paid union president in the country. He earns only about ten

The late Senator Robert Kennedy offering bread at the end of Cesar Chavez's twenty-five-day fast in 1968. Left to right: Helen Chavez, Senator Kennedy, Cesar Chavez, Juana Chavez, Cesar's mother.

dollars a week, although he works fourteen hours a day. As UFW president, he is involved with overall planning and strategy, training local leaders, and forming helpful political alliances. He also tries to increase public understanding of issues of concern to the union as he speaks to groups, walks picket lines to support worker protests, and fasts when he feels that is necessary.

Cesar Chavez and one of his grandsons

The eight Chavez children are grown and there are twenty-four grandchildren. The oldest son, Fernando, is now an attorney who has served as president of the Mexican American Political Association. Daughter Linda is married to a member of the union's national executive board, while Anna and Elizabeth and their husbands are active in the Democratic party. Sylvia is married to a fire fighter, and Eloise's husband manages a Delano grocery store. Anthony and Paul are both with the union, Anthony as a communications technician.

Cesar Chavez remains optimistic for the union's future. He has pointed out that workers were able to organize in the 1960s, despite many difficulties, and thinks the UFW can overcome present-day challenges. He remains committed to improving the lives of farm workers, whether by fasting, involving celebrities, meeting with politicians, or talking with schoolchildren. He says he loves his job and is grateful that he can make a contribution to helping others.

Since the original edition of this book was published, Cesar Chavez has passed away. Chavez died on April 23, 1993, at the age of sixty-six. More than forty thousand people attended his funeral. He is buried in La Paz, California.

Henry Cisneros

The house on the west side of San Antonio was once owned by Romulo Munguia, a man who had escaped from Mexico in the 1920s after being sentenced to death for political reasons three different times. The same house has been occupied by a mayor of San Antonio, Henry Cisneros, and his family. Henry Cisneros enjoys his home, the neighborhood, and the ties to the past, for Romulo Munguia was his grandfather. Family history and values helped form the career of Henry Cisneros, a major voice in American politics and a leader of the nation's ninth largest city.

Part of Henry's family history was shaped by events in Mexico. Many families, including his mother's, chose to leave their country during the early 1900s, a time of political unrest. Henry's maternal grandfather, Romulo Munguia, originally lived in

Mexico. He was an orphan by the age of eight, worked in print shops as he grew up, and he was directly affected by political events. Romulo worked in one shop which printed a newspaper opposing Mexican President Porfirio Díaz. When the shop was raided by police, he was arrested, jailed, and even sentenced to death—the first of three times this happened because of his political involvement. That first time he was pardoned and released because of his young age, only eighteen. By 1915, Venustiano Carranza, a leader he supported, was in power. Mr. Munguia published a newspaper and was an alternate delegate to the Constitutional Convention of 1917. Life was more peaceful then, and he married Carolina Malapica. But in 1920, Carranza was overthrown and killed. In January, 1926, Mr. Munguia fled his home, just a day before soldiers came looking for him, and crossed the border into Texas.

San Antonio attracted many Mexican refugees, and there Romulo once again worked for a newspaper, and he soon made enough money to send for his wife, three sons, and daughter, Elvira. He later started his own business, known as Munguia Printers, and promoted business, cultural, and educational ties between the United States and Mexico. The family lived comfortably in San Antonio.

Near the end of World War II, Elvira met George Cisneros, just back from military duty in the Pacific. The two had been introduced by her brother Ruben, and after a traditional courtship, George and Elvira

married. George's ancestors were early Spanish set-
tlers and, even before the American Revolution,
lived in what is now the state of New Mexico. For
generations, George's family had farmed and
ranched, but when the property was divided,
George's father did not inherit enough land to support twelve children. After his mother died, George
became a migrant worker with his father, who eventually bought a small farm in Colorado. Realizing
the importance of education, George graduated from
high school and business school and went to work
for the U.S. government. He was also active in the
Army and retired with the rank of colonel in the
Army Reserves. Both Romulo Munguia's activities
and George Cisneros' dedication to government service and the military would greatly influence a member of the next generation in the family, Henry
Cisneros.

Henry Gabriel Cisneros was born in San Antonio
on June 11, 1947, the first of five children for George
and Elvira Cisneros. As parents, they wanted their
children to work hard and continually improve
themselves. Henry remembers childhood as "tre-
mendously enjoyable." He says, "I had chores, piano,
and reading. During the summer, my brothers, sisters, and I competed in branch library competitions
and tried to stay at the top." His parents limited
television, so during the week the children were only
permitted to watch programs such as *National Geo-
graphic* specials and the news. Outings were often

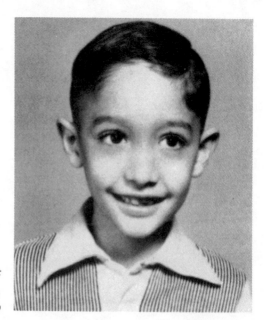

Henry Cisneros in first grade, Little Flower School, San Antonio

educational. The family would visit museums, classical music concerts, or even the railroad station to learn about trains. Henry's life also included many friends. He recalls, "I grew up in a neighborhood full of children. There were sixteen boys my age. We played football and baseball in the street. It was a tremendous neighborhood life."

Henry did well in school. He skipped third grade and was always young for his class thereafter. While at Central Catholic High School, he was in the Reserve Officer Training Corps (ROTC). He planned to be an Air Force pilot, influenced by his father's military career and his interest in aircraft. However, Henry graduated from high school at sixteen, and

LEFT: *Eight-grader Henry Cisneros, Little Flower School*

RIGHT: *Henry Cisneros in his ROTC uniform, Central Catholic High School, San Antonio, 1964*

only received an alternate appointment to the Air Force Academy, so he enrolled at Texas A&M University. Although he would not become a pilot, he still pursued his military interests. Henry found Texas A&M challenging in the classroom and enjoyed the discipline and competition in the Corps of Cadets. He was also involved in many other activities, including the "Aggie" band, and distinguished himself as a school leader.

Henry started out majoring in aeronautical engineering, but changed his career direction when he had trouble with calculus, an advanced math. He had been selected to attend a conference to be held in West Point, New York, for student leaders from all over the country. He was impressed at how the other students were so well informed on current events and issues. He also visited New York City and realized the importance of good city management to a city, its people, and even the nation. Since Henry had always wanted to serve his country, he decided to achieve this goal by solving urban problems. He would work with the same dedication and discipline he had always displayed. In 1968, he graduated from Texas A&M with a major in city management and, according to a brother, the desire to become the mayor of San Antonio.

After graduation, Henry earned a master's degree in urban and regional planning and worked in city administration. Back in San Antonio, he became assistant director for its Model Cities Department.

This was a program begun at the federal level to help some cities with their problems. Poorer city residents were to participate in the program's decisions, and citizen councils were organized. Henry Cisneros gained real experience in the workings of government. He also learned about San Antonio's politics with its different interest and citizen groups.

During this period Henry married Mary Alice Perez, whose family owned a grocery store near the Cisneros home. The two had met at a baseball game when he was fourteen and she was twelve. They both had strict parents and had not been permitted to date until he was a senior in high school. After their marriage in June, 1969, Henry and Mary Alice moved into a garage apartment in San Antonio, but within six months they prepared for a move to Washington, D.C. Henry had been accepted into a doctoral program at George Washington University where he could learn more about administrative and monetary aspects of cities—financing, taxes, budgets.

Once in Washington, Henry was hired as an assistant to the executive vice president of the National League of Cities and worked toward his next degree. The Cisneros' first child, Theresa, was born. In 1971, Henry was one of sixteen people chosen from a field of three thousand applicants to become White House Fellows. He worked as an assistant to Elliot Richardson, then Secretary of Health, Education, and Welfare. Mr. Richardson helped him realize the importance of politics in solving cities' problems. He also advised Henry to return to San Antonio and develop a political base in his own hometown.

Before returning to San Antonio, however, the Cisneroses moved to Massachusetts because Henry had received a Ford Foundation Grant to attend Harvard University. He earned a second master's degree there, in public administration. Then he went to the Massachusetts Institute of Technology (MIT) where he was a teaching assistant and finished the course work for his doctoral degree. In addition, he completed the dissertation he had begun at George Washington University. He received his doctorate in public administration from George Washington University in 1975, and Henry became Dr. Cisneros. Meanwhile, the family had moved once again, but this time it was back home to San Antonio.

Henry Cisneros became an assistant professor in the public administration program at the University of Texas at San Antonio and began his political career at the same time. He ran for City Council on the ticket of a political organization comprised mostly of businessmen. Ruben Munguia (Henry's uncle who had introduced George and Elvira Cisneros and who now ran the Munguia print shop begun by his father, Romulo Munguia) was active in this group and helped get Henry on the slate. Less than a year after the family's return home, Henry Cisneros won his first election. At age twenty-seven, he was the youngest councilman in San Antonio's history. Another happy event for the Cisneroses was the birth of their second child, Mercedes Christina, just a month after the election.

Dr. Cisneros served as a councilman from 1975–1981. He worked with business persons and developers, as well as with Communities Organized for Public Service (COPS), a Mexican-American community action group. He wanted to bring new technical industries to San Antonio and he wanted to improve the lives of the poorer residents. The city was involved in a controversy over its election system. Councilman Cisneros was one of those who voted to change the "at-large" system to a "single-member district" system, which would give minorities a better chance of electing representatives. In the next election, minority candidates won a majority of council seats.

When Henry Cisneros ran for mayor in 1981, he had the backing of many business persons and many who were less prosperous. Supported by Mexican Americans as well as members of other ethnic groups, Henry won the mayoral contest by nearly 62 percent of the votes cast. In 1983, he was re-elected by a margin of almost 95 percent, and was reelected again in 1985 and 1987.

Henry Cisneros has described his job as mayor: "[It is] to keep the city moving forward. I lay out projects, help create jobs, keep spirits high, and address principal problems. I must be open and accessible to everyone." He would often walk the streets of the city to hear the concerns of its residents.

San Antonio is the nation's largest city that has a majority of Hispanic people. Under Mayor Cisneros, San Antonio benefited from much planning and development. During his first term, he began "Target '90," a project in which over five hundred citizens defined 150 goals for the city to reach by 1990. Technological industries, such as computers, relocated in San Antonio. It is fast becoming a center for biosciences. A $200 million shopping plaza and expansion of Paseo del Rio—the city's famous Riverwalk—was built, and Sea World of Texas (complete with Shamu the whale) opened in 1988 as the world's largest aquatic park. The mayor even tried to get a National Football League expansion team for San Antonio. Such projects attract tourists, create jobs for the residents, and bring tax money to the city.

On occasion, Mayor Cisneros was criticized for being too interested in developing big and visible projects, such as a domed stadium (referred to as the Alamodome), at the expense of providing better education or job training for residents. However, Henry Cisneros feels that economic development is needed before many of the city's problems can be solved. He lists major accomplishments as "the opening of Sea World, the revitalization of downtown San Antonio, and the sense of progress. San Antonio was previously thought of as slow; now it is characterized as dynamic."

The nation has noticed Henry Cisneros as a mayor

Mayor Henry Cisneros, San Antonio, Texas

and as a leading Hispanic politician. He gained much attention when he served on the National Bi-Partisan Commission on Central America appointed by President Ronald Reagan. He publicly disagreed with the Commission's conclusions. When former Vice

President Walter Mondale ran for president in 1984, he considered Mayor Cisneros as a possible vice-presidential running mate. In 1987, Henry Cisneros disappointed numerous people when he announced he would not run for governor of Texas in 1990. The mayor declined to enter the race because his newborn son, John Paul Anthony, had a heart problem and would require much care. A year later, in September, 1988, Henry Cisneros stated that for personal reasons, he would not seek a fifth term as mayor.

While Henry Cisneros is primarily known for being a politician, he has also held other positions. Since the job of mayor pays so little, he has earned most of his income from lecturing and teaching. He says that at the college level, "I help young people understand the nature of public administration . . . Case studies approximate the setting and time limits and pressures on the job. The students enjoy learning realistically." Additionally, Henry Cisneros has been active in working toward a National Hispanic Agenda, a program of goals which could be supported by different Hispanic groups, including Mexican Americans, Cuban Americans, and Puerto Ricans. He has served as president of the National League of Cities, on the Board of Trustees of Notre Dame University, the Board of Regents of Texas A&M University, and on many such boards and commissions. He continued his military activities until 1978, when he resigned as a captain in the Army Reserves.

Henry Cisneros says that his daughters have been affected by his positions and experiences. "They have begun to show positive goals and leadership potential. Theresa was president of her junior class at high school, is a member of the swim team, and makes excellent grades. She competed in a city-wide oratory contest and won a trip to Pennsylvania, and has visited the Soviet Union. Mercedes, who is on the honor roll, is a cheerleader and leader in her class. They have a sense of commitment and are highly motivated." Henry Cisneros values time with his family, including his parents who still live close by. He also enjoys jogging.

When asked about the inspirations for his political career, Henry Cisneros did not hesitate. "My grandfather gave me a sense of public service, my father quoted MacArthur's [a famous World War II general] speech on 'duty, honor, country.' I still have a record of it and listen to it." In order to achieve goals, Henry Cisneros says he "sacrifices normality" and he speaks of having little free time. "I must be single-minded. To have this job you must enjoy the work because you will do lots of it! You must be available to others and sacrifice your own wishes. You must be patient to strike a compromise. You must strike a different attitude with respect to scheduling time. You must be directed to work and be productive most of the time. But you don't mind because you are fulfilled and productive!"

Patrick Flores

At one time, Archbishop Patricio (Patrick) Fernandez Flores was known as the "Mariachi Priest" because of his unusual church services, which included music with mariachi bands and sometimes, afterwards, a fiesta and dancing. Always he has been known as a leader of change. He has protested a violation of civil rights on the steps of the Justice Building in Washington, D.C., been kidnapped at machine gunpoint from a bishops' conference in Ecuador, marched in a picket line at a San Antonio supermarket encouraging people to look for the United Farm Workers labels when buying grapes or lettuce, asked Fidel Castro face-to-face to reconsider the release of political prisoners in Cuba, raised and distributed over $20,000 to Mexico's earthquake victims against the president of Mexico's wishes, and has taken action to improve the standards of living among the poor. His dedication to helping others as the first Mexican-American bishop in the United States has created feelings of new inspiration and confidence for many Hispanics.

Patrick F. Flores was born the sixth of nine children on July 26, 1929, in Ganado, Texas. His parents, Patricio and Trinidad Flores, were both from southern Texas and believed that through education and hard work their children could rise to a better life. The Flores family farmed on land owned by a wealthy family. They shared in the profits of the harvest in payment for use of the land. During the winter months, they lived in a small house without running water or electricity.

During the summer and fall months, the Flores family would pack the pickup truck and trailer with living necessities (including his mother's washing machine and stove) to follow the migrant trail from area to area with the farm workers harvesting rice and picking cotton. This was a difficult way of life, working from dawn to dusk and often living in sheds or barns.

The Flores children helped their parents in the fields, and when traveling, their schooling became sporadic or they sometimes missed most of the regular school year. Patrick's parents reminded them of the importance of learning and to do the best they could do. Patrick remembers that some encouraging teachers would give them books and assignments to take with them, but after a long day's work and often no electricity in their shelters, it was almost impossible to read and study at night.

Because of few opportunities to stay in one school or in one area for any length of time, it was not easy for the Flores children to form friendships or to gain acceptance. Patrick Flores has not forgotten how, in some small rural towns, he was not allowed to enter certain restaurants, swimming pools, movie theaters, or roller rinks because he was Mexican American. It was these experiences which later prompted others to say of him that he has never lost his understanding and feeling for people with similar circumstances.

In the early 1940s, the Flores family moved to Pearland, Texas, where they obtained a bank loan to buy farming land and build a house. This was a more permanent home base, and it was during this time that Patrick's desire to enter the priesthood, as well as his leadership qualities and good communication skills, began to develop. One of the first people to recognize Patrick's abilities was a young father, a newcomer to Pearland, whose children attended the same Mexican-American school that Patrick did. This school was only one room, with no running water and one teacher for all grade levels. The Mexican-American children walked over a mile to their school, while Anglo children were bussed to a more modern school with one teacher for each grade.

The young father organized a group to protest this situation and asked Patrick to become the sec-

Patrick Flores at age fifteen, Pearland, Texas

retary. He thought Patrick was an especially good listener and a hard worker. Patrick taught himself to type, in order to help organize and write letters to raise funds for this group's cause. Eventually they were able to change the system so that all Pearland students attended the same school. An Hispanic attorney, also working for this cause, was so impressed with Patrick's talent in letter writing and his ability to direct fund-raising groups that he offered to send him to law school. But young Patrick had a different future in mind.

The next person to take notice of Patrick's talents was the priest who came to their town, periodically, to hold church services in a tent. Patrick worked with the priest. Soon the priest saw that Patrick had the knack of holding an audience's interest when he spoke and that he had a certain self-confidence about himself. Because the priest was not there every day and the nearest church was close to twenty miles away, Patrick began to hold his own religious classes for friends at his home. In his early teen years, he started with only ten children and after a few years had almost sixty children attending his classes.

When Patrick Flores made up his mind during his late teens that he wanted to become a priest, he was met with discouragement. There were several things that Patrick needed to consider, such as finishing high school (Patrick dropped out to help his family before graduating from high school when his father had become ill), entering the seminary (a school especially for the ministry), how to pay the cost of going to this special school, and how he would be able to live in a different city where he knew no one. Patrick did not give up. Soon after, a nun named Sister Mary Benetia, who had come to Pearland with the traveling priest and taught religion classes, took up his cause. She was able to get Bishop Christopher Byrne to meet Patrick. Impressed with the young man's desire to become a priest, the bishop offered to pay the cost of his schooling at a private high school in Galveston. Patrick must pass every subject, especially Latin, and show his report card to Bishop Byrne every term. Everything began falling into place. The same bishop knew of a family that Patrick was able to live with near the high school. In return for room and board, Patrick helped with the family's shrimping business.

While attending Kirwin High School in Galveston and making up for the schooling he had only sampled as a migrant farm worker, Patrick Flores would again experience a different outlook on life. He recalls the time that the Pearland police took him from school to ask about a fire at the car dealership where he used to work. The night before the fire, he had organized a dance for the Mexican-American community in Pearland. The dance was held in the large display room of the car dealership. (Patrick was a good dancer. He and his sister had won several dance contests together.) Early the next morning, a fire broke out and the building was a total loss. Someone reported a man who looked like Patrick running out of the building right before the fire. Patrick was arrested for arson and put in jail. He maintained his innocence for one week until his family finally found him. He was released and not charged. Because of this experience, Patrick Flores has visited prisons across the nation and tries to help those who come to him feeling that they may have been wrongly accused.

Patrick Flores finished the rest of his schooling with excellence. He studied at St. Mary's Seminary in La Porte, Texas, and was ordained a priest in 1956 at the age of twenty-seven. He became assistant pastor of a church in Houston. The pastor of this church did not allow Patrick Flores to speak Spanish, even though several of the Mexican-American church members were more comfortable speaking in their native language. The pastor's directive was difficult for Patrick to understand. However, this situation

led him to the Cursillo religious movement that was
to influence his own style and methods as a priest.
The Cursillo movement started in Spain. It com-
bined religion with music, and a simpler and more
personal style of religious service. Also, the services
were conducted in Spanish, and it brought many
Mexican Americans back to the Catholic church.

Patrick Flores was the pastor of his own church
in Pasadena, Texas, for a while, and then was assigned to a church in Houston where he became
known for his Cursillo style of church services. It
was during this time that Mexican Americans began
to be recognized as a group not to be overlooked
within the Catholic church. In the late 1960s, Francis
Furey was appointed as the new archbishop in San
Antonio, Texas. Archbishop Furey was sensitive to
the Hispanic majority in the population that he
served and submitted Patrick Flores' name for aux-
ilary bishop. Patrick Flores became the new bishop
in San Antonio and the first of Mexican-American
descent. Because of this, he also became the "unof-
ficial bishop" to all Hispanics in the United States.

Patrick Flores has played an important part in less-
ening some of the problems that Mexican Americans
face. In the early 1970s, he visited Cesar Chavez in
a Monterey, California, jail. Chavez had been jailed
because of his efforts in organizing a farm workers'
union for improved working conditions. In addition
to speaking out in support of migrant farm workers'
lettuce and grape boycotts, Patrick Flores also spoke

Patrick Flores ordained as bishop, May 5, 1970

out for clothing manufacturer workers of a major company who went on strike for better wages and the right to form a union.

During his career, Patrick Flores has helped to found or lead different organizations with the purpose of helping others, especially Hispanics. One of these groups was called "Los PADRES" (Priests Associated for Religious, Educational and Social Rights). The goals presented to the Catholic church included more Spanish-speaking priests assigned to Spanish-speaking areas, consideration for selecting Mexican Americans for the position of bishop, acknowledgment of Hispanic language, food, and customs. The second goal was fulfilled by the Catholic church with the appointment of Patrick Flores as bishop, and the last was accomplished by Archbishop Furey and Flores together. They established the Mexican-American Cultural Center (MACC) in San Antonio, dedicated to help Hispanics to prepare for leadership roles in American businesses and communities and to help others to understand their Mexican-American heritage. A few years later, the National Hispanic Scholarship Fund (NHSF) was founded by Patrick Flores to assist Mexican Americans wishing to study for the priesthood or other professions, as he once had. As president of NHSF, he is responsible for awarding yearly scholarships totaling over $1.2 million to Hispanics in higher education. In addition, he is a supporter of Communities Organized for Public Service (COPS), a founder of the Office of Catholic Services for Immigrants, and chairman of the Texas Civil Rights Commission. The sum of these achievements became evident to the nation when he was recognized as one of "200 Rising Leaders" of America in the July 15, 1974, issue of *Time* magazine.

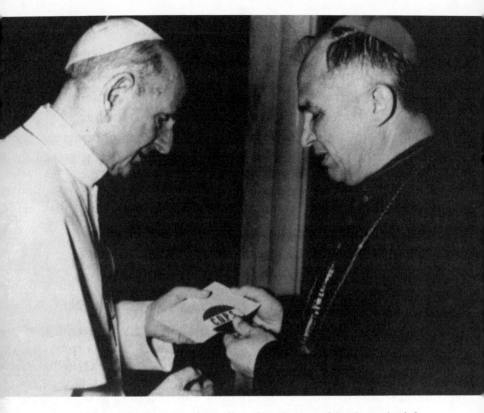

Flores with Pope Paul VI discussing Communities Organized for Public Service (COPS)

In the late 1970s, Patrick Flores was assigned as bishop to El Paso, Texas. His stay was suddenly interrupted when Archbishop Francis Furey passed away and Flores was named to follow him as Fourth Archbishop of San Antonio. At this time Patrick Flores reflected upon the main people who were responsible for his rise from a migrant farm worker to the great honor of being Archbishop of San Antonio. These were his parents, Sister Mary Benetia Vermeersch (the nun of his early religion classes who first took up his cause), and Archbishop Furey who had appointed him as auxiliary bishop of San Antonio.

In 1987, Pope John Paul II made an historic journey to the United States. A few years earlier, Archbishop Patrick Flores hand-carried an invitation to Rome asking Pope John Paul to come to San Antonio. He also spoke with the Pope about the growing Hispanic community in the United States and

Pope John Paul II and Archbishop Patrick Flores, San Antonio, 1987

how it affects the Catholic church. Pope John Paul chose to stop in San Antonio during his nine-city visit to the U.S., welcoming and recognizing the importance of Hispanic communities. He addressed the public gathering in San Antonio in the Spanish language. On the morning that Pope John Paul left San Antonio, Archbishop Flores gave him a special send-off. The Pope was entertained by mariachi bands along the road, from the Archbishop's residence where John Paul was staying to Kelly Air Force Base where he departed.

As Archbishop, Patrick Flores ministers to over half a million people in San Antonio, Texas. His popularity and dedication to change are well known. He has said that he believes in meeting problems in a straightforward manner and will speak out and act against inequities. His work will continue to be felt, clearly and directly, by the Catholic church and by society in the years to come.

Dolores Huerta

"When I was teaching school and gave it up to organize farm workers, the other teachers I worked with thought I was crazy. Later on, though, they thought it was wonderful." Dolores Huerta still considers her position wonderful. She is first vice president of the United Farm Workers and its highest-ranking woman.

In the 1600s, Dolores Huerta's ancestors settled in what is now New Mexico. She was born Dolores Fernandez in Dawson, New Mexico, on April 10, 1930. Her father was a mine worker and also a farm worker. Dolores remembers that when she was five or six, the family migrated and moved from one area to another to follow the harvesting of crops.

After Dolores' parents divorced, her father stayed in New Mexico and she lived with her mother in

Dolores Huerta, about age five, in New Mexico

California. Her mother worked in a cannery and as a waitress. She saved enough money to open her own business, first a restaurant and then a hotel. As a child, Dolores was active in the Girl Scouts and the church choir.

Dolores says that she felt little discrimination during her childhood, either as a girl or as a Mexican American. "I was raised with two brothers and a mother, so there was no sexism. My mother was a strong woman and she did not favor my brothers. There was no idea that men were superior. I was raised in Stockton in an integrated neighborhood. There were Chinese, Latinos, Native Americans, blacks, Japanese, Italians, and others. We were all rather poor, but it was an integrated community so it was not racist for me in my childhood.

"My best girl friend was of Chinese descent and Buddhist. I learned about her religion and she learned about mine. I went to all the Chinese festivals with her and still remember the Chinese New Year's Eve banquets. That day, every year, I would come home from school, go right to sleep, and then wake up in time for the banquet which began at midnight.

"I started noticing racism as a teenager and it took a long time to overcome the feelings. We were treated differently and it was a bitter and hurtful experience. I was treated badly because I was poor, Mexican American, and a girl. But it prepared me for later life. I became very angry against discrimination. 'Be yourself' was always my mother's advice, and it helped, especially in high school.

"There were many decisions made in high school to exclude the poor and minorities from activities. I was in a club that was planning a school dance. They wanted fancy decorations for the dance and to charge three dollars to get in. This was more than they had to charge. Three dollars was a lot of money back then, and many could not afford it for a dance. I thought it was too much and suggested they charge less. Some others in the club said that if they did not charge as much as three dollars, many students would think the band they hired was no good. They did not care that poorer kids could not go.

"After that dance experience, I quit the club and felt terrible pressure. It became hard for me at school. There was a contest to see who could sell the most war bonds. A trophy was to be awarded to whoever had sold the most bonds. I was the one who sold the most, but I never received that prize. I think they could not face the fact that a Mexican-American girl had sold the most. As another example, I loved to write poems and compositions and was good at it. In one of my classes I got all *A*'s on my papers and tests, but I received a *C* for the class. I asked the teacher why, and she said that she thought my work was too good and that someone had to be writing the papers for me! I was crushed."

Her awareness increased: "I was a teenager in Stockton and there were fields all around. My mother had a hotel, and most of the people in the hotel were

Dolores Huerta
in her teens

farm workers. I saw their plight and heard their complaints of low wages. They would work so hard and earn so little. Their wages were about sixteen dollars for two weeks' work." There were also *braceros*, laborers from Mexico who were brought in to work in the fields. Dolores says that her mother often let poor farm worker families stay at her hotel for free, and that she would also try to help *braceros*.

While growing up, Dolores had wanted to be a Spanish dancer, and she studied music and dance. She gave up this dream, though, when she married her boyfriend at the end of high school. They had two girls, but then the marriage broke up. Dolores' mother took care of the young children as Dolores earned a degree so that she could teach.

While still living in Stockton in the early 1950s, Dolores met Fred Ross. He was setting up chapters of the Community Service Organization to help Mexican Americans. By organizing, they could register voters, elect Hispanic representatives, and improve their lives. Initially, Dolores was skeptical of Fred Ross because his promises sounded too good to be true. Eventually, she realized that Fred Ross was sincere and that the CSO could help Mexican Americans gain power and effect changes. She has since credited Fred Ross with changing her own life and its direction.

Dolores' first job with the CSO was voter registration. She later became a lobbyist, a person who tries to influence lawmakers on behalf of a special interest. She tried to persuade legislators in Sacramento, California's capital, to help with the work of the CSO. She lobbied for the right for people to take a driver's license test in their own language, disability insurance for farm workers so that they would still get some money if they were physically unable to work, the right to register voters in their homes instead of making them come to a courthouse or central location, and the end of the *bracero* program. Dolores' work in Sacramento gave her valuable legislative experience.

In 1962, however, Dolores left the CSO to help

Cesar Chavez in his attempts to organize the farm workers. She had first met Cesar Chavez in 1955 when he, too, was working for the CSO. He had quit the CSO, also in 1962, when they discouraged him from trying to unionize the migrant workers because so many past efforts of that type had failed. At first, Dolores helped organize farm workers near Stockton and Modesto, but Cesar soon requested that she work at the group's headquarters, then in Delano, California. At that time the organization was called the National Farm Workers Association (NFWA).

While still with the CSO, Dolores had remarried, to Ventura Huerta, and she had more children. When Dolores began her work with the NFWA full-time, she was concerned about the welfare of her children. Although housing, food, and a clothing allowance were provided, officials such as Chavez and herself received only five dollars a week. She knew that she would be working hard and traveling extensively. Fortunately, she could rely on the union's living arrangements. It was like an extended family. Union families helped each other in caring for children, just as grandparents, aunts, and cousins would. At times, daughter Lori supervised the younger children, and son Emilio would stay with Cesar and Helen Chavez. At other times, some of the children would accompany Dolores, and daughter Alicia remembers hearing stories during the long drives. Dolores knew that this living arrangement might be difficult for them, but she feels that the separations and any hardships helped the youngsters better relate to the more serious difficulties of others. Lori remembers that her mother always said, "Now you are sacrificing a little, but you are helping thousands of farm workers' children a lot."

Cesar Chavez, Dolores Huerta, and others with the NFWA had many goals. They wanted the farm workers to be free to vote for the union's help and they wanted the union to be able to bargain effectively with the growers. They wanted the workers to control and improve their own lives. They hoped to get higher wages, better living conditions, and a safer work environment. In many fields, chemicals were used to prevent crop damage, but the union questioned the health effects of these pesticides. The union also wanted to be able to provide benefits for the workers, such as health insurance to pay doctors' bills. They also wanted to stop growers from using *braceros*, who were paid less money and labored under poorer conditions than domestic farm workers. The NFWA felt that the union should be guided and funded by the farm workers themselves. And they wanted to operate without violence.

Dolores marched on the picket line when the National Farm Workers Association called its first grape strike in September, 1965. When workers refuse to work, the employers usually are forced to deal with the workers' complaints. But the grape growers could simply hire other nonstriking workers, so the strike was not effective. The NFWA then turned to a more powerful method to pressure growers: the grape boycott.

During a boycott, people do not buy or use the product, and therefore put pressure on the producers to change their ways. During the boycott, Dolores negotiated contracts with some of the grape growers, but the pressure continued against others. The grape boycott involved people all over the country who were sympathetic. Church and civic groups in cities as far away as New York joined in. In the winter of 1967–68 about fifty farm workers made the long trip to New York City, and Dolores Huerta was the boycott coordinator on the East Coast for the next two years. Her family was scattered; some of her children lived with her in New York, others stayed in California. Son Vincent remembers attending high school in Manhattan. Daughter Lori says she spent time touring with Luis Valdez and his theater troupe, Teatro Campesino, to raise money for the boycott activities. In 1970, the union was victorious. More contracts were signed and many benefits were gained.

By this time the National Farm Workers Association had become associated with the AFL-CIO and soon its name was officially changed to United Farm Workers of America (UFW).

For Dolores, the striking, boycotting, negotiating, and lobbying have come in cycles. She was involved in various lettuce strikes and contracts, and she lobbied a great deal. In 1985, she appeared before the House of Representatives' subcommittee hearings. She testified against a plan permitting foreign workers to temporarily enter the United States to harvest crops which spoil quickly.

When asked about her present responsibilities, Dolores Huerta replied: "My duties are policy making, like Cesar Chavez. It is the creative part of the organization. I am in charge of political and legislative activity. Much of my work is in public relations. I speak to a group every week or two. My honorarium, or speaking fee, always goes to the union." That particular day she would speak at a college graduation. "What I like most about my job is to be able to change things for people, to change things for the better."

Dolores married Richard Chavez, Cesar's brother, after being divorced from Ventura Huerta. (She still uses the name Dolores Huerta in her professional life.) Dolores and Richard live at La Paz, the site of UFW headquarters in Keene, California. Dolores has eleven children: Celeste, Lori, Fidel, Emilio, Vincent, Alicia, Angela, Juanita, Maria, Ricky, and Camila. The oldest and youngest are twenty-six years apart. Some of the children still live at La Paz, while others are grown and have families of their own. As they were growing up, Dolores knew their lives were difficult because of her work, but now she is confident that all has turned out well. "Now they are tough, political, responsible, and loving."

Nancy Lopez

Most of her children have been involved with the union, distributing leaflets as youngsters, working in different departments as adults. Now most have left their official union work, but she is very proud of the lives they have chosen. Today, one son is a busy doctor who takes time to help the homeless. Another is an attorney, one "followed his grandmother's talents and is a chef," a daughter is studying to be a nurse.

Some of her children admit that while growing up, their lives were often disrupted, but they say they know their mother always cared. She tried to do her best for the farm workers and for them. Now she also makes time for her grandchildren.

When asked how she would like to be remembered, Dolores Huerta replied, "I would like to be viewed as a woman who cares for fellow humans. We must use our lives to make the world a better place, not just to acquire things. That is what we are put on the earth for."

Nancy Lopez

 "The ultimate goal for professional golfers is to get into the Hall of Fame. There are only eleven women who have achieved this honor. In other Halls of Fame, you are usually selected by a committee for how you played and what you have done for your sport. But in the LPGA [Ladies Professional Golf Association] Hall of Fame, you are admitted based only on performance. It probably has the strictest requirements and is the hardest to achieve."

Nancy Lopez was entered into the LPGA Hall of Fame after winning the Sarasota Classic in 1987. She has won almost every major championship title and broken almost every record set at the amateur, collegiate, and professional levels. Nancy Lopez is the first and currently the only Mexican-American golfer to compete in the Ladies Professional Golf

Association. What is her present goal?

"To keep breaking records that I set for myself and to win as much as possible. There is one record I haven't broken and that is Kathy Whitworth's record of winning eighty-seven tournaments during her career. I have won thirty-nine tournaments in ten and a half years, but the competition is much tougher now. There are several strong competitors playing in the LPGA today that make winning a greater challenge."

Nancy Lopez was born to Domingo and Marina Lopez on January 6, 1957, in Torrance, California. Soon after, the Lopez family with Nancy and her older sister, Delma, moved to Roswell, New Mexico. Here, Domingo Lopez opened his East Second Body Shop and his wife worked with him as the shop's bookkeeper.

In the early 1960s, Marina Lopez became ill and was told by her doctors that walking would be good for her health. Domingo Lopez enjoyed the game of golf and began to play with his wife, who benefited from the therapeutic exercise by walking the course. Nancy would often accompany her parents and to keep her from getting bored, they would let her hit the golf ball every so often. Her father gave her a Patty Berg four wood (a golf club used to hit the ball long distances) which he sawed off for this special gift. (Patty Berg was one of the founders of the LPGA and was its first president and member of the Hall of Fame.) Soon Nancy's parents took notice of their daughter's golfing ability. Despite being so small, she was able to hit the ball long distances toward the hole with accuracy. Soon after, Nancy received her own set of golf clubs.

Nancy's career began when she was nine years old by winning a "peewee" tournament. By the age of twelve years, she had played in three state women's tournaments and won one. In addition, she won the New Mexico amateur title, the Mexican Amateur Tournament, the U.S. Golf Association Junior Girls championship (twice), and the Western Junior title (three times). While growing up, Nancy was coached by her father to become a professional golfer. He discouraged her from using her hands for anything but golf, and did not allow her to wash the dishes. Nancy noted, "I did not do any dishes because the warm water would soften the calluses [hardened spots] on my hands. I played so much golf that if my hands were too soft it would hurt to hold the golf clubs for so long. My father did not let me do dishes, but he saw to it that I did everything else!" It was also important to her father that she get braces for her teeth because he knew that she would one day become a public figure.

During this time, Nancy's mother and father influenced her greatly, but in different ways. "My father never told me that I had to play, but he helped and encouraged me to play happy and to do my best. I did more things with my father than my mother. We played golf, went hunting together—I didn't shoot any guns, but walked with him—and we went to baseball games. My mother was also supportive of my golf. She would pick me up everyday after school and take me to the golf course to practice. I would change clothes in the car on the way over! She influenced me in the feminine way. I remember that she told me I shouldn't wear jeans on the course, so I wore golf skirts. These skirts were short and one time in a tournament I was bending over in an unlady-like way and she took me aside to tell me how to bend over correctly. I was such a tomboy!"

Nancy was a member of Godard High School's otherwise all-male golf team. She led the team to the state championship and earned the number one ranked position as an individual golfer. "At first the boys on the team weren't sure if they liked a girl playing, but they ended up liking me. It was the other teams (all-boy) that we played against that had a problem with me!" When playing in tournaments with the golf team, she did not use the ladies' tees, always the men's. (Ladies are usually allowed to hit the first ball at each hole from a spot twenty yards closer than men.) One of her special accomplishments in her senior year at Godard was to place second in the Women's Open. But golf was not the only sport Nancy participated in. She was the "all-around athlete" who played flag football and basketball as well as partaking in gymnastics, track, and swimming. Nancy belonged to the local Girl Scout troop and was active in her high school's service

Young Nancy Lopez

organization. It was about this time, Nancy recalls, that her sister, Delma, twelve years older, introduced her to music like Chubby Checker and the Twist.

In high school Nancy always enjoyed math and wanted to pursue a degree in engineering, but golf was still a high priority. The University of Tulsa recognized Nancy's talent as a golfer and offered her an athletic scholarship. She took engineering courses and played a great deal of golf. Again, she built a long list of achievements. In her second year at college, she won amateur and collegiate titles and was chosen Most Valuable Player and Female Athlete of the Year for golf at Tulsa University. Also, she was a member of the Curtis Cup and World Amateur teams.

At the end of her second year in college, Nancy was faced with a difficult decision. She had always liked school and was able to play in many tournaments. However, when she was younger she sometimes had to sacrifice doing things with her friends or miss out on special field trips because of her golf. In college, she fell behind in her studies, even with the tutors who helped her. Tournaments, traveling, and practicing her golf were taking up almost all of her time.

"I decided I had to see if I could make it on the pro tour. I felt I had grown up a lot in two years and my golf game was ready. As an amateur and collegiate golfer, I had done the maximum and came to a dead end with golf. I thought if I leave, I could always come back, but I had to try.

"I also worried about how lonely it would be going from tournament to tournament, week after week. I didn't want to grow old playing golf. I'm old-fashioned. I wanted a husband and family and wondered if I could ever meet someone special without staying in one place for long."

At the age of nineteen, Nancy became a professional golfer. Joining the Ladies Professional Golf Association (LPGA), she made a very successful debut. During the late 1970s, she is remembered for five impressive wins in a row and was recognized as Rookie of the Year, Player of the Year, and the fourth woman player to earn more than $200,000 in one year. At one time, early in her professional career, she had won more than $800,000 and was ranked seventh on the All-Time Career Money list. She also was awarded the Vare Trophy, given for having the lowest average golf scores. She became very popular among the press, and the public enjoyed following Nancy's exciting career.

The 1980s brought a transitional period for Nancy Lopez. Her marriage to television sportscaster Tim Melton ended, and she decided upon some new goals. She began by losing over twenty pounds and keeping herself on a strict diet. Nancy Lopez explains that she works hard to maintain her weight and weighs herself in the morning and evening each day.

She says that she will sometimes pack an apple or raisins in her golf bag for an energy snack, but otherwise eats only breakfast and dinner. Exercise is also very important to Ms. Lopez and, in addition to practicing her golf two or more hours a day (even when she is ahead in a tournament), she tries to include aerobics in her daily schedule.

In 1982, Nancy Lopez married Ray Knight, a professional baseball player then with the Houston Astros. Ray Knight has mainly filled the third baseman's position for over eleven major league seasons. He has been a member of the Cincinnati Reds, Houston Astros, New York Mets, Baltimore Orioles, and more recently, playing third or first base with the Detroit Tigers. His strongest batting season so far was with Cincinnati and he was named Most Valuable Player as the Mets third baseman in the 1986 World Series. Both Nancy and Ray have been married before and agree they bring a special understanding to the almost daily demands put upon professional sports stars. They feel their strong religious beliefs also help to reinforce the relationship. About a year after their marriage, their first child, Ashley, was born.

Ashley Knight has probably traveled more miles than most children her age. She has been able to accompany her mother on the road at tournaments across the nation. Nancy has commented that the one part of her marriage to Ray that she cannot get used to is their sometimes long separations. His team will play "away" games and when they return home it may be time for Nancy to play in one or more out-of-town tournaments. However, they would not have it any other way if it meant one of them quitting their careers and being unhappy. It was during this time that Nancy Lopez had one of her best years. She topped the money list with over $400,000 by winning five tournaments over the 1985 season and was named Woman Athlete of the Year by the As-

Nancy Lopez
after a tough shot

sociated Press. At the end of this season, Nancy Lopez announced that she was planning to have another child. A second daughter, Erinn Shea, was born the following year.

Nancy again joined the LPGA tour with Ashley, Erinn, and their nanny by the summer of 1986. Her typical day while on tour is an exhausting one.

"It's hard with children, but I'm fortunate to have a full-time nanny, so I can take the girls on tour with me. Most of my tours are two to three weeks, but sometimes we are away from Ray for three to four weeks. Before the tournament even begins, I pack fourteen to fifteen suitcases, strollers, toys, diapers, and I have to rent a van just to get to the hotel from the airport! My day begins very early when the girls are still asleep. I practice first and by the time I'm finished playing golf, it's just about dinner time. I eat with the children, play with them for a little while, then put them to bed. Sometimes I barely have enough energy after a long day in a tournament.

"Our tournament season runs from February to October and part of my job also includes making guest appearances, filming commercials, shooting advertisements, or doing charity tournaments for my sponsors. This may add up to about three weeks in total days, but it's spread out over the year."

The 1987 season was a momentous one for Nancy Lopez. The book, *Nancy Lopez's The Complete Golfer*, that she coauthored with Don Wade was published. This book followed an earlier one, *The Education of*

"It is important to me to be a pleasant person."

a Woman Golfer, that she wrote in 1979. Secondly, Nancy Lopez became the eleventh player to join the world's best women golfers in the LPGA Hall of Fame. To qualify for this prestigious honor, she was an LPGA member in good standing for ten consecutive years and won thirty-five official tournaments, including one major championship. The Hall of Fame building is located at the Sweetwater Country Club in Sugarland, Texas. Nancy Lopez has earned a permanent exhibit there which displays photographs of her ten-year career, a brief description of her life, and a video showing her championship golfing style.

"As a professional athlete, I hope I will be remembered as one of the best lady pro golfers. And I would want people to know that I have always been sincere in what I felt or talked about. When I was fifteen years old, I was trying to get an autograph from a professional athlete. He was rude and put out by the crowd of fans, and that left a lasting impression with me. I thought then that when I became a professional athlete I would not want to be like that—not an egomaniac. It is important to me to be a pleasant person and I really appreciate having lots of fans!"

Nancy Lopez Knight does have many fans and is proud of her success. Her religion, family, and superstar career all add up to a very fulfilling life.

Vilma Martinez

When attorney Vilma Martinez was invited to speak to a group of eleventh- and twelfth-grade students, she heard them commenting about her résumé. It detailed her impressive career, which had included the top position at the Mexican American Legal Defense and Educational Fund (MALDEF) and the chairmanship of the Board of Regents of the University of California. Ms. Martinez decided to tell her audience about how she really achieved her degrees and positions. "I talked about how I put myself through college and had very few dates. I had one lipstick at a time and did not wear the latest fashions. I also talked about the hours of boring, meticulous preparation which goes into legal work, and into preparing a court case for a few moments of glamor."

Ms. Martinez wanted to let the students know

about all the preparation that led to her success so that they, too, would work hard. She believes the rewards have been worth the effort. She has used her belief in education and in working within the system to help Mexican Americans as a group and to achieve her own goals as an individual.

Vilma Socorro Martinez was born October 17, 1943, in San Antonio, Texas. Her father, Salvador, was a construction worker. Vilma was the eldest of five children, and she had to care for her younger sisters and brothers. Vilma was the one to be punished if they disobeyed a rule, such as not returning home on time after playing. While this taught her responsibility, it also made her think that she would never want children of her own.

The Martinez family lived in an integrated neighborhood with Mexican Americans, blacks, and whites. Vilma says, "Trust was not based on prejudice. Each person was individually evaluated." Her neighborhood background influenced her later life because she became concerned about civil rights and because she feels "equally at ease" with different races.

There was another important part of Vilma's background which also helped her. She was raised for years by her grandmother, who was a very strong person, and Vilma never believed that women had to be weak or passive. Also, Vilma's grandmother taught her to read and write in Spanish, even before she started school, and this gave Vilma confidence in herself.

There was no kindergarten, and Vilma directly entered the first grade. Initially, school was a shock because classes were taught in English, and Vilma knew no English. There was an assumption by some that the students who did not know English were not as smart, but Vilma knew she was. She knew that since she had learned to read and write in Spanish, she could also learn English, and she did.

Vilma's first-grade teacher was an older woman, Miss Butler. "She lined up the children and did not let them go home until they had recited the lesson of the day." Vilma remembers how Miss Butler took great pride in her job and took education seriously. She respected Miss Butler.

Vilma enjoyed school and was a good student. Her fifth-grade teacher used her paper as a model to grade others. One day Vilma made a mistake which the teacher did not notice, and all the other papers had that mistake marked as correct! She recalls, "I loved to read and read a lot. I loved biographies, what people did and how they dealt with crises. I kept my interest in reading when I was older, and enjoyed *Catcher in the Rye.*"

During childhood, Vilma encountered discrimination, but she overcame it where she could. Her junior high school counselor recommended that she go to a vocational or technical high school, just because she was Mexican American. Vilma objected and was permitted to attend an academic high school. Vilma has said that she had no professionals as role models while growing up in a poor neighborhood, other than secretaries and teachers. At fifteen, however, she worked a summer for Alonso Perales, one of her father's friends. He was a lawyer and Vilma was impressed by how he could help people. "He helped a couple adopt a child; he helped a young widow whose husband was killed in a crop dusting accident." Vilma decided that she, too, wanted to be an attorney.

When Vilma announced that she wanted to go to college, her parents acted in a way she could have predicted. She said that her mother was always encouraging, while her father was skeptical. He said that she "would not complete school, that she would get married and have children." As she looks back, Vilma says, "I know he was a loving man and probably just wanted to spare me disappointment, since he did not get a college scholarship for himself." Her father's opinion did not stop Vilma. On the contrary, it made her more determined and she worked harder. She says that her father's discouragement also provided her with early training in advocacy, which is arguing for a cause. She would later use this ability as an attorney.

Vilma's high school counselor refused to advise her how to apply for college, so she wrote to the University of Texas for application forms herself.

Once at the University of Texas, she was anxious to graduate, and she finished in two and a half years. Her knowledge of Spanish helped her complete college. When she needed just two more credits to finish, she noticed a course in conversational Spanish and "just talked" to satisfy the requirement. Vilma graduated in 1964. She majored in government, with law school in mind, and decided on Columbia University in New York City.

At Columbia, Vilma says that she felt discrimination as a woman, but again she resisted. During an interview for a scholarship, the interviewer asked why she should be considered when she would probably marry and have children instead of practicing law. Vilma replied that she had not worked that hard for so many years not to practice law. He recommended her and she got the scholarship. Vilma graduated from Columbia University with a law degree in 1967. While studying for the New York Bar examination, which must be passed before a lawyer can practice in that state, she met Stuart Singer, who was also preparing for that test. They were married in 1968.

Vilma Martinez had learned to overcome discrimination and low expectations. She was succeeding for herself, and she wanted to use her legal talents to help others. She had decided to specialize in civil rights and her first job, from 1967–70, was with the National Association for the Advancement of Colored People (NAACP) Legal Defense Fund. She handled cases involving discrimination against race and sex. She also helped another civil rights group, one which was just forming, get private grant money. This new organization would become the Mexican American Legal Defense and Educational Fund, better known as MALDEF. Next, Vilma worked for the New York State Division of Human Rights. Her job concerned employment discrimination.

In battling discrimination, Vilma realized that there were many obstacles for Hispanics. When she heard that the head of MALDEF was resigning, she applied for his job. Based on her skills and reputation, Vilma Martinez was appointed president and general counsel of the Mexican American Legal Defense and Educational Fund in 1973.

MALDEF had begun in San Antonio in 1968, with only three attorneys but with money from the Ford Foundation. One of its goals was to file "class action" suits—ones which benefit a whole group of people—so that Mexican Americans could gain economic, political, and social advantages. Another MALDEF goal was to increase the number of Hispanic attorneys in this country. By 1973, MALDEF had grown and had six offices: in San Antonio, San Francisco, Los Angeles, Washington, D.C., Albuquerque, and Denver.

As president and general counsel for MALDEF from 1973 to 1982, Vilma Martinez was concerned about selecting cases, training attorneys, raising money,

Vilma Martinez, MALDEF President and General Counsel, 1973-82

and insuring that legal judgments were obeyed. She wanted MALDEF's cases to settle issues which would provide equal access to education, voting, and employment for all Hispanics. She knew that MALDEF had to make sure that decisions in court cases were actually put into practice. She spent much time traveling and raising money, and accomplished her goals by working through the system, with whomever was in power. She feels that MAL-

DEF means that Mexican Americans have their own institution to insure that change occurs for them.

During the nine years that Vilma Martinez was with MALDEF, many important civil rights were won. In 1974, bilingual education was guaranteed for all children who did not speak English and attended a public school. In 1982, the United States Supreme Court decided that undocumented children, like all children, had the right to a free public education in Texas. In still another case, the decision ruled that the state legislature in Texas could not be elected "at-large," a practice which weakened the voting power of any minority. Henry Cisneros was a member of the San Antonio City Council when it was sued by MALDEF in a similar case, and he, too, was opposed to the "at-large" system. Ms. Martinez said that they met for the first time during this lawsuit and that she found him "a very pleasant and impressive person."

While Vilma Martinez headed MALDEF, the budget went from $800,000 in 1973 to over $2.6 million in 1982. The staff more than doubled. MALDEF continues to help Mexican Americans.

Since May, 1982, Ms. Martinez has been a courtroom lawyer. She is a partner in a large private law firm in downtown Los Angeles, and handles legal proceedings in federal and state courts. Her clients are companies such as Pacific Telephone, Blue Cross, and Allstate.

Vilma Martinez's career experience and dedication

have led to many important activities. Under President Jimmy Carter, she served on the Advisory Board on Ambassadorial Appointments, helping to select ambassadors to represent the United States in foreign countries. She is active with The Achievement Council, which helps poor and minority students prepare for college. She also serves on the boards of the Southwest Voter Registration Education Project (SVREP), which was directed by William Velasquez, and of the Anheuser-Busch Companies.

Vilma Martinez is also on the Board of Regents of the University of California, which has nine campuses. In 1976, California's governor, Jerry Brown, suggested Ms. Martinez for a position on that board. She was supposed to travel to Sacramento, the state capital, for the interview. However, she was expecting her first child at any time, and so the interviewers came to her. She received final notice of her appointment soon after her son Carlos was born. In 1984, she was elected board chairman, and after a two-year term she resumed her regular position on the board. She is pleased to serve the University because she believes that a fine education is very important.

With her successful career, Vilma Martinez has also had a busy family life. When she was young, she thought that she never wanted children, but she later changed her mind. She and her husband, also an attorney, have been married over twenty years

*Vilma Martinez, member of the Board of Regents,
University of California*

and have two sons, Carlos and Ricardo. At times, Ms. Martinez (who uses her maiden name professionally) admits that being a working mother is not easy. "I have to miss certain parts of the children's lives—a birthday, a school open house. I try to compromise, although sometimes that is difficult. I must adhere to the court schedules—the judges, opposing lawyers, the schedules of witnesses, trial dates." She feels sad about missing some time with her children. However, she does not feel guilty, because she thinks that practicing law makes her a better person and therefore a better mother. She says her younger brother James has been a big help. He lived with Vilma and her husband from his junior high through college years, and he has been a third adult for their sons. She says that family life is also a bit easier with private practice than when she was with MALDEF.

In looking back over her life and career, Vilma Martinez says that all has not been easy, but it has certainly been worthwhile. She knows there has been progress, but she says that we, as a country, will have to work on several issues. One is "securing the elusive birthright of equal protection under the laws." Another issue concerns education. "Education is very important. It prepares you, and you equip yourself to help others. It gives you the tools to compete." She thinks more money should be spent on all levels, from preschool through college. A third issue which deeply troubles Vilma Martinez is discrimination. "I am skeptical if someone says there is no discrimination." She knows too well that there is. She was forced to suddenly learn English in the first grade. At one job, her boss wanted to take her out for lunch at his private club, but she was not accepted there. More recently, she was wheeling her son in a stroller near their home when she met a new neighbor. He complimented her on her English, assuming she was a maid and caring for her employer's child. He did not imagine that she was the boy's mother, or a homeowner, or a prominent attorney.

Vilma Martinez has proved that she could succeed despite discouragement. She has worked hard and speaks openly of sacrifices as well as success. "Things have their prices and we must pay the prices. As head of MALDEF there was a big price, but it was very important. The job took energy and skills. I traveled 50 percent of the time, missing my children. But," she emphasizes, "there are no regrets! I feel proud and privileged to have served."

Luis Nogales

On October 17, 1943, a caravan of cars, filled with farm workers, followed the crops. As they passed through Madera, California, one pulled to the side of the road. Florencia Nogales was about to give birth. Luckily, her mother, who had delivered other babies, was present. A son, Luis, was born. Years later, this story would be told in the plush surroundings of a corporate office, high above Los Angeles, with a limitless view. The office belonged to Luis Nogales and he delighted in sharing his rise from the fields to the corporate world. Much like his parents, Luis Nogales did start out harvesting the crops, but then his life began to change and he went on to graduate from Stanford Law School, was selected as a White House Fellow, and served as president of United Press International and then Univision Spanish Language Television Network. What pleases Mr. Nogales, even more than his own success, are the opportunities he has had to help others and the ties he has maintained with his relatives, old friends, and culture.

Luis Nogales says that his parents gave him the spirit that led to his successes. The Nogaleses wanted their children to have better lives than they had as farm workers. Florencia had been born in Mexico and her husband, Alejandro, was born in Los Angeles, but they were both raised in southern California. Luis says, "My mother was determined and wanted her children to improve their opportunities. My father had a fourth-grade education, but he had a love of learning." His father bought books on literature, history, and philosophy in both Spanish and English. Luis remembers that his was one of the few migrant families that traveled with their own small library of books. Florencia and Alejandro were concerned about their children's self-images. The family moved from Delano as a home base to Calexico, a California town next to the Mexican border. The Nogaleses wanted their children to see across the border and realize that Mexicans had many professional jobs, that they were not just farm workers or laborers. They wanted their children to realize that race was not the reason for poor jobs in the United States, that there were other reasons. They championed the idea of civil rights for Mexican Americans to their children. At a young age, Luis was told by

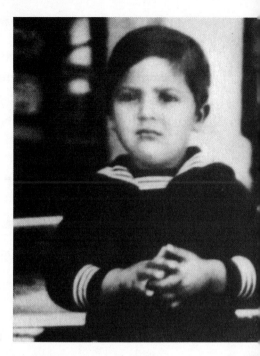

Luis Nogales, about age four,
Calexico, California

his father that he would be a lawyer if he studied
and worked hard. He also knew he would work for
the rights of Mexican Americans.

The four Nogales children all went on to finish
college, but there were times when their education
had to wait, as they earned money for the family.
Luis remembers that while staying in Manteca, California, the family lived across from the country
school they attended. "There were four grades in a
room; each row was a different grade. We went to
that school while our parents were working at the
local cannery with tomatoes and fruits. Our father
got hurt. A row of boxes fell on his leg and it was

almost amputated. He was laid up, so we had to be taken out of school to pick grapes. It was a hard time. Every morning there was a 'cheering section' from the school as the kids watched us leave for work. The school was happy when we came back."

During his school years, Luis had many jobs. "I mowed lawns, shined shoes, had a newspaper route, delivered milk, and worked at a golf course. I even played hooky to go to the golf course to work. I was always earning money, but I gave most of it to my parents. With my own money, I bought useful presents for my mom. We were almost at the survival level during most of my childhood. There was no money for frivolities, just necessities."

Luis almost failed his freshman year in high school. He had all *D*'s and *F*'s the first semester, but then he improved. During his junior year, he had his first Mexican-American teacher and was inspired by this role model. "On graduation day, the biggest store in town offered me a job, but my father refused for me and said I would be a lawyer. My mother wondered whether I should accept and work in an air-conditioned place and wear a shirt and tie—an improvement from working in the fields."

During the summers, Luis did farm labor along with many of his friends and relatives. He recalled, "Each year was tough money-wise." Luis helped organize farm workers so that they could gain more rights. He did not like the way the farm workers were treated or how they were made to feel helpless

*Luis Nogales, high
school graduation*

and inferior. Years earlier, he had heard of Cesar
Chavez and his efforts. Luis wanted to help the farm
workers, but did not want to remain in agricultural
work. "I had self-confidence. I never doubted that I
would be an attorney."

Luis went to San Diego State University in the
1960s on a scholarship. This was a time of awakening
Chicano activism on many campuses. Luis helped
found and organize Mexican-American student
groups at college. He graduated with a degree in
political science, and continued his studies. One reason he chose Stanford for law school was because

his family had picked fruit in the area. His father would point out the campus and hope aloud that one of his children would attend. While at Stanford, Luis continued to help minorities. He founded MECHA (a Mexican-American student group) and was involved in tutoring, boycotts, advocating admission of minorities and hiring of Chicano administrators and professors, and organizing meetings at dorms. Changes resulted at Stanford. There was an increase in Chicano admissions and a Chicano Studies program was started.

In law school, Luis learned to analyze and negotiate—abilities which were important in his career. He also learned about leadership and the importance of working effectively with influencial people. At the same time, he continued his ties to his family, old friends, and culture. During the summers, he worked with the crops until his last year in law school. He did not think that he had to choose between his future career and his heritage. "Some fellow students at Stanford seemed troubled. They thought if Chicano, then they should not be at Stanford; if at Stanford, then they were not Chicano. This is not a choice you have to make. You can be a successful Chicano who helps his community."

Luis Nogales received his law degree from Stanford in 1969. In his first job after graduation, his philosophy about cultural ties and his ability to negotiate came into play. He acted as a liason between Mexican Americans at Stanford and the university itself, with the title of Assistant to the President of Stanford. He helped Chicanos be part of Stanford while still keeping their own identity. He worked with the administration to set up policies and programs to benefit Chicanos.

From Stanford, Nogales went to Washington, D.C., as a White House Fellow, and worked as an assistant to the Secretary of the Interior. His experience had been limited to California, but he knew that Washington was an important center. "Being there you actually see how it is in the capital for international politics. Major international and national decisions are made every day." He met many important officials and also took some fascinating trips as part of the program. He traveled in the Soviet Union and rode the train across Siberia during the winter. He recalled how the Soviets would wet the outside windows of the cars as the train pulled into a station. The windows would instantly be coated with thick sheets of ice and the passengers were prevented from seeing anything outside the train. In March of 1973, he was in one of the first American groups to visit China after President Richard Nixon "opened" relations with that country. He also traveled to Pakistan, Bulgaria, Poland, and East Germany. He was exposed to many different governments and all types of people. Luis says that his experiences at that time really affected his outlook and prepared him for his future career, especially his position at United Press International.

In 1973, Luis Nogales was hired by a television station in Los Angeles to direct its business and legal affairs. He soon became a vice president for the conglomerate that owned the station, Golden West Broadcasters. The company owned other television and radio stations and a major league baseball team, the California Angels. During the seven years Luis was at Golden West, he used his negotiating talent. He helped his company buy more stations, worked out legal agreements for programs and talent, and labor contracts with the employees.

Luis Nogales has also used his ability to negotiate outside his regular job. In 1975, the University of California asked him to help settle a dispute at the Santa Barbara campus between the administration, minority faculty, and a group of students. Luis visited the campus, determined to resolve the disagreements. Some people were surprised when he was successful in just five days. What they didn't know, he later said kiddingly, was that he took only five days' worth of clean clothes in his suitcase.

As his career developed, Mr. Nogales continued to serve the community as well as private companies. He began to take positions on a number of boards and commissions. During the 1970s, he joined the boards of both the Mexican American Legal Defense and Educational Fund (MALDEF) and Levi Strauss, a maker of blue jeans. He also was vice chairman of a California Commission on Post Secondary Education and the Los Angeles Community Redevelopment Agency. He worked briefly at his own public relations firm, and then joined a large national agency, setting up a division specializing in the Hispanic market.

By this time, Luis Nogales had a reputation for being effective in negotiation, business, and the communications industry. All those capabilities would be needed in his next job, at United Press International (UPI). The company had been founded in 1907 by newspaper magnate Edward Scripps, but the news service had a history of financial trouble. The Scripps company kept it operating until 1982, then sold it. The new owners wanted to make UPI profitable, and in 1983 they hired Luis Nogales as an executive vice president to help them.

UPI gathered and sold news reports and photographs to newspapers and television and radio stations around the world. The wire service had 2,000 employees, about 3,000 part-time writers and photographers, and 269 bureaus all over the world, but it had not shown a profit in twenty years. Luis Nogales became president in 1985, and worked with employees as well as with creditors so that UPI could survive. He and many others felt that the public was best served by having two news services, both UPI and its rival, Associated Press (AP). They knew that UPI was a valuable news agency worldwide, and Mr. Nogales cited its leadership position in gathering and distributing news in Latin America.

In 1985, UPI filed for Chapter 11 bankruptcy in

order to solve its financial problems. Under Chapter 11 a company continues to operate as it develops a plan to pay its debts, while the bankruptcy court supervises and legally protects it from its creditors. Luis Nogales was named chairman and chief executive officer, and continued to reorganize and refinance UPI under the direction of the bankruptcy court. He prepared the company for sale. UPI had survived, and the following year it was purchased by a Mexican newspaper owner. Mr. Nogales felt that his job with UPI was finished and he soon resigned.

Luis Nogales' next job was with Spanish language television. The parent company, Univisa, was owned by a Mexican businessman. It operated in the United States and some Latin-American countries. All together, it had 409 affiliate stations. Mr. Nogales was first hired as president of Univisa's news service. He added two new regular newscasts to *Noticiero Univisión*, produced in Los Angeles and broadcast nationally. The news service gave priority to news about U.S. Hispanics and news of interest to them.

In 1987, Luis Nogales was promoted to president of the television network, by then called Univision. Under his leadership, the network's operations were strengthened, favorable publicity was gained, and sales grew. Hallmark bought Univision in 1988, and Mr. Nogales announced the purchase agreement and also that he would resign following the sale.

Luis Nogales admits that he had no master plan for his career. "I think you cannot plan a career, only your education." He feels that a person has to be "ready, open, and flexible." He thinks that too many children do not even try because they are afraid to fail. Luis Nogales has seen his jobs as challenges. He admits that at times he has been scared, "But when I am entirely comfortable, I know it is not anything challenging. Great athletes always have 'butterflies in their stomachs.' " He said that his mentors, more experienced people who guided him, always helped him, especially in difficult situations. He feels that he has a responsibility to be a mentor to others who are still rising.

Mr. Nogales says that his success did not come without certain sacrifices or hardships. He gave up a certain security in moving from job to job. Although his travel has recently decreased, he flew over 250,000 miles in a particular two-year period. He also mentioned that he is divorced.

Through his experiences, Mr. Nogales has formed definite opinions about our country. "As I traveled and worked with people from different countries, I am even more convinced that this is the greatest society in the world today for people to better themselves and achieve. I believe in reform as the way to change and improve society." He thinks there are many opportunities for people to help in different ways. Corporate decisions affect the quality of life in our country, just as civil rights groups do. He says that each person should be involved however they can.

Luis Nogales continues to serve on the boards of Stanford University, Bank of California, and Lucky Stores. He hopes that one day his own daughters, Maria Cristina and Alicia, will surpass even his success in their own ways.

Luis Nogales has been at the top of corporations, and at the same time he has helped the community. He has worked with many important and famous people, while he also maintained contact with old friends. "Just because a person is successful, they don't abandon the past. My parents still live in Calexico. I still consider it my hometown and I frequently return. I walk by the area where day laborers wait, because I know and have worked with many of them. Many of my relatives are still farm workers. I never totally leave the past."

Luis Nogales with daughters Maria Cristina and Alicia at Notre Dame Cathedral, Paris, 1987

Edward James Olmos

 What do Jaime Escalante, El Pachucho, Gregorio Cortez, and Lieut. Martin Castillo all have in common? Edward James Olmos—actor, singer, dancer, director, and musician. They are all characters he has portrayed in theater, movies, or on television, and they are well known to millions of viewers. Olmos is a unique individual who is committed to high goals in both his personal and professional life.

Edward James Olmos was born in East Los Angeles, California, to Pedro and Eleanor Olmos on February 24, 1947. Eleanor's family has lived in Los Angeles for at least three generations. Prior to coming to the United States from Mexico, some of her relatives fought in the Mexican Revolution. Her mother's grandparents were revolutionaries and owned a controversial but popular newspaper in

Mexico City. Pedro Olmos and Eleanor Huizar met in Mexico City while Eleanor was visiting a sister. Pedro was a businessman in Mexico City from his early teenage years. In 1945, Pedro came to Los Angeles to marry Eleanor. Olmos says of his father, "He could not speak English and there were some very hard times. He first went to work in a slaughterhouse but couldn't do that for long because he was too small. So he became a welder."

Edward Olmos grew up in the Boyle Heights area of Los Angeles with his older brother, Peter, and younger sister, Esperanza. He describes his neighborhood as a western Ellis Island (the island in New York Harbor where people from Europe first entered to settle in the United States). There were people of different races and religions—Hispanics, Native Americans, Koreans, Chinese, Japanese, Mexicans, Russians, Jews, Mormons, Baptists, and Jehovah's Witnesses. "It was a fantastic environment," he has said.

During the mid-1950s, Edward Olmos moved to Montebello (about ten miles east of downtown Los Angeles) with his mother when his parents divorced. He became an eager baseball fan and player. He feels lucky that it was baseball he enjoyed at that time and not drugs, alcohol, or smoking. He practiced every day of the week to become the best baseball player he could. He watched professional baseball players to see what he needed to do to improve himself. Then he would practice until he mastered the new

LEFT: *Edward Olmos in his Little League uniform in 1956*

RIGHT: *Portrait of Edward Olmos at age ten*

skill. His self-disciplined training paid off. In his early teen years he was catching for a Los Angeles Dodger pitcher who often worked out during the winter months at the Montebello ball park.

Although separated from his family, Pedro Olmos went to Edward's games and remained a part of his son's life. He introduced an enjoyment of music and dancing to young Edward. Edward describes his father as a quiet person, but not on the dance floor. Pedro Olmos taught his children how to two-step, jitterbug, cha-cha, and dance the dances of the 1940s. Edward taught himself to sing and play the piano, and by the early 1960s, he formed the Pacific Ocean band.

By the mid-1960s, Olmos had graduated from Montebello High School and was performing with the Pacific Ocean at popular nightclubs on Hollywood's Sunset Strip. He claims he was a better dancer than a singer. During this time, he was learning to open up and express himself. He discovered how to be a master of ceremonies and how to create a relationship with his audience. He sang and danced and was sometimes a stand-up comedian.

School was a top priority in Edward Olmos' life. He attended East Los Angeles Junior College and California State University at Los Angeles during the daytime and performed with the band at night. He often worked on class assignments during his breaks because he knew the advantages of having an education. He signed up for dance and theater classes to improve his showmanship, and discovered that speaking words with emotion is often easier than singing them. He became more and more interested in acting and approached this with the same self-discipline that he used with baseball, singing, and dancing.

By the early 1970s, Edward Olmos was supporting a family with earnings from small television parts. He met his wife, Kaija Keel, at one of his Hollywood nightclub performances. They were married in 1971. Kaija Keel is the daughter of Howard Keel, the famous movie actor who has played the role of Clayton Farlow on the television program, "Dallas." Edward and Kaija Olmos have two sons, Mico, whose name is from the Spanish words meaning "my son," and Bodie, who is named after an eastern California ghost town. During this time, television roles in such shows as "Hawaii Five-O" and "Kojak" kept the Olmos family going, but on a strict budget. In between acting jobs, Edward Olmos would sometimes take other jobs like delivering furniture. However, he continued his learning by working with small experimental theaters and taking acting workshops in the Los Angeles area.

One day in the late 1970s, Edward Olmos tried out for a part in Luis Valdez's play, *Zoot Suit*, which eventually propelled him to fame. He played the role of El Pachuco who keeps up a running commentary on characters and events throughout the play. The play was based on the "zoot suit riots" that occurred in Los Angeles during a time of racial tension. The riots followed the "Sleepy Lagoon" murder trial of 1942 in which several Hispanic youths were convicted amidst great controversy. As El Pachuco, Edward Olmos dressed the part. He wore the zoot suit of the 1940s—baggy pants with wide legs and tight cuffs, a long suit coat, a hat with a flat top and wide brim, and a watch chain that can be seen hanging from the pants. He later went to New York to perform as El Pachuco on Broadway and also did the 1982 film version. He was honored by receiving the Los Angeles Drama Critics Circle Award, and a Tony Award nomination for his extraordinary performance as El Pachuco.

The early 1980s brought different film roles for Edward Olmos, such as *Wolfen, Blade Runner,* and the public television special, *The Ballad of Gregorio Cortez. The Ballad of Gregorio Cortez* was a true story about a man of Mexican descent who was accused of killing a sheriff and who became part of one of the largest manhunts in the history of Texas. Cortez became a wanted man because of a mistake in translating one word from Spanish to English. He was able to escape the Texas Rangers for several days over hundreds of miles on foot and horseback until he was finally caught. He served many years in prison before being granted a full pardon by the governor. Edward Olmos recognized Cortez as a true Hispanic

Olmos in the movie The Ballad of Gregorio Cortez

hero. So that the audience could fully appreciate Cortez's story, Olmos spoke only Spanish throughout the film.

During the almost five years that Edward Olmos dedicated himself to making and promoting *The Ballad of Gregorio Cortez*, he remained very selective about the parts he accepted. It was important to him that any contract he signed was not exclusive, allow-

ing him to work on other projects. Although understanding that money is a necessary part of life,
he could not lose sight of what was truly valuable
to himself and his goals.

Michael Mann, producer, learned of Edward
Olmos' integrity when offering him the part as Lieut.
Martin Castillo on the popular television show,
"Miami Vice." Olmos insisted upon and was granted

*Olmos as Lieut. Martin
Castillo in "Miami Vice"*

the freedom to do other work. His role as the intense, quiet, and complex police lieutenant has earned him an Emmy for Best Supporting Actor in a Drama Series (1985) and the Golden Globe Award (1986).

One of the other projects that Edward Olmos completed while a part of the "Miami Vice" cast was the film *Stand and Deliver*. He earned a 1989 Oscar nomination of Best Actor for this role. Edward Olmos played the teacher, Jaime Escalante, who helped eighteen unmotivated high school students to pass a difficult test in calculus for possible advance college credit. To give these students, who were from gang neighborhoods, a college level test was thought by many to be senseless. When they passed, the Educational Testing Service questioned the results. The students took the test again and passed with the same or higher scores. Jaime Escalante taught his students, believed in their abilities, and refused to listen to those who tried to discourage him from reaching his goal. Through this film, Olmos and Escalante present role models to Hispanic youth, indicating that they are able to achieve whatever they want if the desire is great.

Free time for Edward Olmos is mostly spent on speaking tours, charity work, and his family. He is committed, like Jaime Escalante, to inspiring young people to keep trying until they get what they really want. For the past several years, Edward Olmos has made time to visit schools, hospitals, libraries, juvenile detention centers, Indian reservations, and prisons across the United States with this message. His wife, Kaija, helps with the many charity requests, answering fan mail, and reviewing scripts for Edward, as well as maintaining two homes, in Miami and Los Angeles. His two sons have had small parts in his films, but his time with Mico and Bodie is often spent going on twenty-mile bike rides. They have even toured up to sixty miles in one day. Music is still an important part of Edward Olmos' life and he also enjoys taking his speedboat out for pleasure cruising whenever he can.

Today, Edward Olmos is developing his own films through YOY Productions, formed with Bob Young. He has worked hard to achieve success, and he looks forward to increasing his accomplishments as actor, director, and role model.

Katherine Davalos Ortega

On September 12, 1983, Katherine Davalos Ortega was nominated by President Ronald Reagan to be the 38th Treasurer of the United States. She is the tenth woman Treasurer and the second Hispanic woman to hold this prestigious position.

Donaciano Ortega and Catarina Davalos were from pioneer families that settled in what is now New Mexico during the 1800s. They married and had nine children. The youngest, Katherine, was born on July 16, 1934, in Tularosa, New Mexico. Her father had many different job experiences. He was named a deputy U.S. marshal at age sixteen, worked at a copper mine in Bent, New Mexico, had a blacksmith shop, and also did carpentry work. Later, the Ortega family owned and operated a restaurant and dance hall in Tularosa, and then a restaurant and a furniture store in Alamogordo, New Mexico. In 1974, Katherine's oldest sister and brother were founders of the Otero Savings and Loan Association. Her sister Ethel has served as chairman of the board since it was chartered.

The family restaurant provided Katherine with the first on-the-job training for her career today. Katherine's father included all of his children in the operation of the restaurant. Initially, Katherine helped in the restaurant by running errands for her parents. Later, she became a waitress and cashier. One of her sisters did much of the management. Katherine remembers that during their dinner hour, her brothers and sisters would meet to discuss family business. Everyone had an equal say in what was going on and in what he or she felt needed to be done. Katherine believes that her family, especially her father and sister Ethel influenced her career the most.

The importance of education was instilled in the Ortega children by their father. He believed that an education gives you a strength within yourself that cannot be removed. Katherine attended schools where often Spanish was not spoken. With the support of her family's values and pride in her heritage, she went to school regularly, learned English, and received awards for perfect attendance.

In the late 1950s, Katherine Ortega graduated with honors from Eastern New Mexico University with a degree in business and economics. She also completed studies in secondary education and had considered teaching high school business courses. However, Katherine was told that being Hispanic would interfere with her application for a teaching position in eastern New Mexico. Discrimination, as Mrs. Ortega has noted, is an unfortunate circumstance that needs to be overcome. She accomplished this by embarking on a business career.

Katherine became licensed as a certified public accountant in California. She worked for Peat, Marwick, Mitchell & Company as a tax supervisor. A few years later, the Pan American National Bank of Los Angeles recruited Mrs. Ortega to be vice president and cashier. With her accounting background and her bilingual abilities, she was able to work with the local Hispanic community. This bank had over fifty employees and about $30 million in assets.

In 1975, Katherine Ortega was selected to be president and director of the Hispanic-owned Santa Ana State Bank. She became the first woman president of a California bank.

In the late 1970s, Katherine Ortega returned to New Mexico. She became a consultant to her family-owned Otero Savings and Loan Association of Alamogordo. This bank was organized by her sister Ethel Olsen, who sold her accounting practice in 1974 to begin this venture. Since 1975, Otero Savings and Loan has grown and was recently named among the best performing savings and loans in the United States.

Mrs. Ortega's first presidential appointment came

KATHERINE DAVALOS ORTEGA **101**

in 1982, when Ronald Reagan named her to his
Advisory Committee on Small and Minority Business Ownership. She was later appointed and confirmed by the United States Senate as a commissioner
on the Copyright Royalty Tribunal.

In 1983, while still serving on the Copyright Royalty Tribunal, President Reagan recognized Katherine Ortega's exceptional professional abilities and
quiet determination by nominating her to the position of Treasurer of the United States. After con-
firmation by the Senate, Mrs. Ortega was sworn in
on October 3, 1983, by Secretary of the Treasury
Donald R. Regan as the 38th Treasurer of the
United States.

The Treasurer of the United States oversees the
Bureau of Engraving and Printing, the U.S. Mint,
and the U.S. Savings Bond Division. She also serves
as national director of the U.S. Savings Bond Division. The Treasurer supervises 5,000 employees,
manages a budget of over $340 million, and is a
member of the Secretary of the Treasury's senior
staff.

The Bureau of Engraving and Printing is the
world's largest securities manufacturing establish-
ment. The principal product of the bureau is United
States paper currency. Annually, the bureau prints
several billion notes having a face value of several
billion dollars. The bureau also prints other security
documents and United States postage stamps. The
bureau operates twenty-four hours a day and em-

Katherine Davalos Ortega, Treasurer of the United States

ploys 2,300 people. The signature of the Treasurer of the United States appears in the lower left-hand corner of U.S. paper currency. Katherine Davalos Ortega's name has appeared on over 20 billion notes.

The U.S. Mint produces the nation's circulating coins. The act of April 2, 1792, signed by President George Washington, created the first U.S. Mint in the city of Philadelphia, which at that time was our nation's capital. The Mint is now headquartered in Washington, D.C., and has four production facilities—in Philadelphia, Denver, West Point, and San Francisco. The Mint is also responsible for guarding the nation's gold reserves in Fort Knox, Kentucky. During fiscal year 1989, the U.S. Mint will produce approximately 17 billion circulating coins. It also produces commemorative coins. In 1984 and 1988, gold and silver coins were produced to commemorate the United States participation in the Olympic Games. In 1986, gold and silver coins were issued to commemorate the 100th birthday of the Statue of Liberty. Also, in honor of our nation's 200th birthday, special bicentennial commemorative coins were produced as mementos of this important event. As part of her job as Treasurer, Mrs. Ortega has traveled around the country promoting the sale of these commemorative coins.

As the national director of the U.S. Savings Bond Division, Mrs. Ortega promotes the sale of United States savings bonds. Savings bonds are an easy and safe way to save. The market-based rate makes them fully competitive with other available funding instruments. Savings bonds can be purchased at banks and through payroll deduction plans. Mrs. Ortega has helped more people become aware of the advantages of buying savings bonds and has also started the publication of savings bond information in Spanish.

In 1984, Katherine Ortega was chosen to give the

keynote address at the Republican National Convention in Dallas, Texas. At this convention, Ronald Reagan was renominated as the Republican party's candidate for a second term as president. Being keynote speaker at the convention has been one of the most personally gratifying achievements for Mrs. Ortega.

Katherine Ortega has been recognized for her many accomplishments. In 1977, she was awarded the Outstanding Alumni Award by Eastern New Mexico University. She also holds honorary Doctor

Katherine Davalos Ortega's personal autograph on a dollar bill, above her printed signature as Treasurer of the United States

of Law degrees from Eastern New Mexico University, New Mexico State University, and Kean College of New Jersey, and an honorary Doctor of Social Science degree from Villanova University. Mrs. Ortega has also received the National Association of Bank Women Industry Achievement Award.

When Mrs. Ortega's busy schedule allows her time to relax, she enjoys reading and golf.

Blandina
Cardenas Ramirez

 When Blandina Cardenas Ramirez awoke on October 25, 1983, she was going to celebrate her birthday. Instead, she was fired by President Ronald Reagan from her position as a member of the United States Commission on Civil Rights. Dr. Cardenas Ramirez felt she had no choice but to challenge the dismissal. Her decision was based on law and reflected the values she had been taught. She was upheld.

Blandina Cardenas was born in her family's house in Del Rio, Texas, in 1944. She was very small at birth, only about four pounds, and initially it was feared that she would not survive. Blandina had two sisters, six and nine years older than she. Her mother, Amelia Cardenas, recalls that as a child, Blandina was called Bannie, after an equally cherished cousin. She soon began calling herself "Bambi." The nickname has survived, and Dr. Cardenas Ramirez is Bambi, even as an adult.

Amelia Cardenas was a housewife and then worked in a department store. Bambi's father, Rudolfo Cardenas, worked as a butcher. His family had grocery stores and was in the meat business. Bambi says that her father, who had only a third-grade education, "learned to learn from others." Her father's family had emigrated to the United States from Mexico about the time of the Mexican Revolution, and her family had political concerns. "We sat around as a family and talked about politics, philosophy, and the Mexican Revolution, which was the motivation for my grandparents coming." The Cardenases gave their children a pride in their heritage, and Bambi says her parents felt it was important "to develop both languages and enhance skills in both cultures." Bambi knew both Spanish and English by the age of two, and she could read Spanish and English before she entered school. Her parents also "saw themselves as people who open doors, and they were careful that the experience was positive. I remember we were among the first Hispanics to use the swimming pool. I remember going, and slowly the number of Hispanics grew."

Growing up in San Felipe, near the U.S. border with Mexico, also influenced Bambi's life. She never had an identity problem, since both cultures were considered important. San Felipe had a separate school district and the school truly belonged to the community. Bambi remembers that everyone knew the teachers. The superintendent, who was head of the school district, would often give her a ride to school with his own daughter in his red truck.

Bambi enjoyed school and was such a good student that she skipped the fifth grade. She used her abilities to help others. "When aunts born in Mexico decided to become American citizens, I got information and they studied the presidents and Constitution. I was their tutor. These women in their sixties wanted to be citizens because a cousin was running for office and they wanted to vote. I was nine." When she was several years older, she was asked to tutor other students at school. One in particular was a football player who needed help in senior English class. "He excelled in sports. I excelled in academics. Neither one of us thought much of the other, but we became best friends. He had a lot of intelligence, though he did not do well on tests. I even helped him write letters to colleges, and he became a successful college and professional player." Tutoring made Bambi realize that students had "different needs and strengths, and every child had to be given a chance to succeed."

From the time Bambi skipped a grade, she was not just the youngest at home but also the youngest in each class in school. "Always, the youngest develop later. For example, I was the last to be kissed. But I was among the smartest and made up for late development by being superactive. I was in debate

Cheerleaders at San Felipe High School, Blandina Cardenas stand-ing, first row, right

and was student council president. I was not very good at sports, but a cheerleader. I loved poetry and anything that had to do with expression. I did much public speaking." Bambi had learned to use her own best strengths.

Bambi had graduated from the University of Texas with a degree in journalism by the time she was twenty. "I never saw myself as a teacher. That was a traditional woman's role. I did not see myself that way." She took a job in Chicago with the American

Blandina Cardenas
at graduation

Bar Association, since she had an interest in law school.

Rather suddenly, in 1967, Bambi's life changed. "My father was ill in Texas. I needed to return home. There was a family pull." She also had another reason for leaving Chicago. "I had always wanted to make a contribution to improving Hispanics. I woke up early one morning and, lying in bed, realized I did not belong there. I wanted to be in Texas to make a difference. It was just when civil rights were reaching the Hispanic community. My life in Chicago was very mainstream. I knew I had to come back. As I came home, things were beginning to develop. My ability to teach and write enabled me to fill roles. For me, civil rights and education came together naturally."

Back in Texas, Bambi did go into teaching, while her roles in education and civil rights grew. She wrote educational proposals for school systems and they received money to develop programs and train educators. She helped organize teaching in Crystal City, Texas, a town where Chicanos had recently won control of their school system after a boycott and protest of the schools. Events in Crystal City attracted many Chicano rights supporters and strengthened the movement. In San Antonio, she worked with Dr. José A. Cardenas at the Edgewood Independent School District, and together they helped make that system a model for the education of migrant children and those who did not know English very well.

Bambi continued her work in education with bilingual and experimental programs. She worked out programs for children from different cultures and backgrounds. She even helped with the television show, "Sesame Street." At the same time, Bambi continued her own education. She took some courses in San Antonio and then went on to receive her Doctorate in Education at the University of Massachusetts in 1974. She then went to work for Senator Walter Mondale in Washington, D.C.

Dr. Cardenas returned to San Antonio where she developed and directed a center concerned with multicultural education and equal educational opportunity for all children, but in 1977 she went back to Washington. President Jimmy Carter had appointed her to be Commissioner of the Administration for Children, Youth and Families in the Department of Health, Education, and Welfare. She was confirmed by the Senate and sworn in by Walter Mondale, who had become Vice President under President Carter. In her new job, Dr. Cardenas had responsibility for programs such as Head Start for preschool children. Her office also worked with day care programs and against family violence. At age thirty-two, Dr. Cardenas had five hundred people working under her supervision and she managed a budget of nearly $1 billion.

Dr. Cardenas got married during this time and

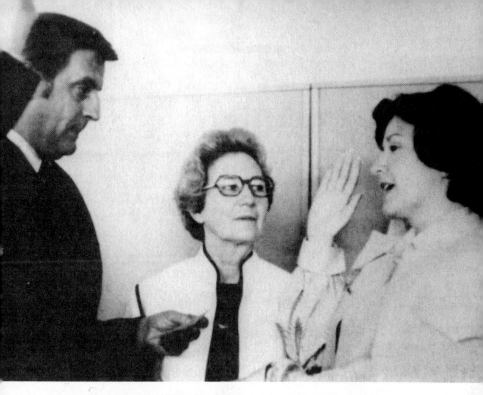

Swearing-in by Vice President Walter Mondale of Dr. Blandina Cardenas as Commissioner of the Administration for Children, Youth, and Families with her mother looking on, 1977

added her husband's name, Ramirez. "I married late, not until my early thirties. Until that time, I thought I would not marry, but that was OK. I had a rich life and marriage was not that important. But I met my husband, we married, and eighteen months later our son was born." Dr. Cardenas Ramirez always thought her work was very important and prided herself in being a strong individual. At times, however, she felt she had to fill certain traditional female roles. Just after her marriage, she ironed her husband's shirt for the first time and admits that she did not do a very good job. Even though she had a successful career and held a high national position, she was still embarrassed, as a wife, sending her husband to work in a wrinkled shirt.

Dr. Cardenas Ramirez had been interested in civil rights for a long time and she had worked for equal opportunity in education. She had seen civil rights hearings in San Antonio in 1968 and was impressed. She felt that the hearings were on important issues, and years later, said, "I remember thinking I wanted to be knowledgeable enough to provide testimony to the Commission, so when I was invited to serve, it was an enormous honor and responsibility." President Jimmy Carter appointed her to the United States Commission on Civil Rights in 1980.

The Commission on Civil Rights was created in 1957. It was to be independent and free from presidential, congressional, or political control. Its job was to make sure that civil rights were not being violated. The Commission could not enforce laws, but served as a watchdog agency to make sure the laws were enforced.

Dr. Cardenas Ramirez served as one of six Commission members, but in May, 1983, President Ronald Reagan announced that he wanted her and two other commissioners replaced with persons of his own choice. The Senate would not agree to this replacement, and five months later, on her birthday, those three Commission members were fired by the

President. Dr. Cardenas Ramirez chose to resist her dismissal. "Not only was the Commission's independence at stake, but there was a serious question about the limits on the power of a president. It was frightening to think I would confront the President, and at the same time I had no choice."

On behalf of Dr. Cardenas Ramirez and another fired commissioner, two civil rights groups, the NAACP and MALDEF, filed a lawsuit to have the dismissals declared invalid and without force. The lawsuit charged that President Reagan had gone beyond his presidential authority and his action affected the power of Congress to create an independent Commission. The suit also said that his action had violated the fired members' own civil rights, since they were entitled to hold their positions under law. With the lawsuit, Dr. Cardenas Ramirez felt that she represented an individual who was challenging the excessive use of presidential power, and that if people did not stand up to power, they could lose rights. If she did not challenge, she thought that she would betray the way she had been raised, and the efforts of those who had "opened doors" in the past. Dr. Cardenas Ramirez wanted the courts to decide the issue. The court decided to reinstate Dr. Cardenas Ramirez and her colleague.

Meanwhile, Congress approved a compromise which restructured the Commission. This new plan defined a Commission member's term as six years, put definite restrictions on the removal of a member from office, and extended the Commission itself until 1989. (It had been periodically renewed by Congress since its creation.) The manner of appointment was changed as the number of Commission members was increased: four members were to be appointed by the President, two by the Senate, two by the House of Representatives, bringing the new total to eight members.

Dr. Cardenas Ramirez was soon appointed by the Senate to serve on the Commission once again. Her position is not a full-time job, but takes four days per month, and she says, "We meet monthly to review the work of the professional staff and make recommendations to Congress and the President on issues concerning civil rights in education, medical care, voting, and the administration of justice." One example of the Commission's work was a 1985 study which compared the income earned by several racial groups to see if the salary difference is caused by racial discrimination or other reasons. In 1987, the Commission commented on a court decision concerning the employment and promotion of women. Although the Commission is due to expire in 1989, Dr. Cardenas Ramirez has said, "I think the Commission will continue to exist. There is a need and general recognition it is needed. It will continue in some form."

Dr. Cardenas Ramirez also has other professional positions and activities. She is the Director of Planning of the Mexico-U.S. Policy Study Program, which is sponsored by the Universidad Nacional Autonoma de Mexico and the city of San Antonio. In August, 1988, she was named Vice President for Institutional Advancement at Our Lady of the Lake University in San Antonio. She is an active public speaker, addressing universities, conferences, and organizations. She serves on many boards of directors, and in the past she has been on the boards of MALDEF and the Women's History Task Force of the U.S. Bicentennial Commission, which planned the 200th birthday celebration of our nation. On a local level, Dr. Cardenas Ramirez worked as Vice-Chair for San Antonio's Target '90 goals, a project of Mayor Henry Cisneros. Dr. Cardenas Ramirez has also been involved internationally as a delegate to a United Nations conference in Denmark, with the Organization of American States in Uruguay, and in visiting China with other educators.

Dr. Cardenas Ramirez says, "There were some sacrifices for preparing for a career and filling it. I never worked on a normal schedule. I manage by cutting back on social activities and setting priorities. There is a high priority on my family." Dr. Cardenas Ramirez does not have much free time, but she commented on another priority. "I make time for learning from others. That's my recreation. I am eager to learn from others—a person doing handiwork or someone at the highest level of business or government. My father believed you could learn from *'Un peon o un presidente'*—a farm worker or a president—and you should respect both equally."

Dr. Cardenas Ramirez spoke of her personal life. She mentioned that her son is already "conscious of the needs of the poor." He is interested in politics, although she says he denies wanting a career in politics. At the age of eight, he wavered between becoming a naturalist or a film producer. She just hopes that he does not abandon the values he has been taught. She wants him to find his fulfillment in both community and global contributions.

Blandina Cardenas Ramirez believes in keeping ties and improving life in the community, but she also feels a person can help on a greater level at the same time. She sees herself as a part of this historical process which helps people. She knows that she, too, has "opened doors," and remembers that her parents always said, "Be the best you can be, not only for yourself, but for others."

Edward R. Roybal

"Before I started school, a man came to the house all dressed up in a three-piece suit. He was a jeweler and he had brought back a watch that he had fixed for my father. But in my mind that man who worked in a suit impressed me so much that I, too, wanted to wear a tie. My mother said, 'That man is wearing a tie because he got an education and became a professional man. And you, if you want to wear a tie all the time, you have to be a professional person and for that you have to go to school.' "

Edward R. Roybal, United States Congressman, started wearing a tie at a very early age because he was committed to preparing himself for his lifework. His political career spans over thirty-nine years, beginning with service in 1949 on the Los Angeles City Council and continuing with his election to the

U.S. House of Representatives in 1962. Since then, he has been successfully reelected each congressional term. During his distinguished career, Edward Roybal has become the senior Democratic member and Chairman of the Committee on Aging, as well as Chairman of the Subcommittee on Treasury of the House Appropriations Committee (the committee that handles the nation's budget). In addition, he also serves on the subcommittees for Health and Education and for Retirement Income and Employment.

Albuquerque, New Mexico, was the birthplace of Edward Roybal on February 10, 1916. He is the oldest child of eight children born to Baudilio and Eloisa Tafoya Roybal. Baudilio Roybal worked for the railroad as a carpenter. He worked at least ten hours a day, but did not wear a suit and tie. At that time, railroad unions were just beginning but were not yet powerful. He went out on strike and when the strike was lost, the Roybal family moved to the Boyle Heights area of Los Angeles. However, before leaving New Mexico, Edward Roybal recalls his start in standing up for something he really believed in.

"My mother bought me a suit with a tie. We went to church every Sunday. In church the kids started to tease me and I got into a fight in the middle of the aisle with a fellow who was kidding me about my tie. We were thrown out of church. My mother was embarrassed—my whole family was embarrassed. But no one as going to take that tie away from me! It goes to show you what a great impression that jeweler had made on me."

In Los Angeles, Edward Roybal attended public schools and graduated from Roosevelt High School in East Los Angeles. During this time he had a paper route and worked at a cleaning plant after school. Young Edward continued to wear his tie and, he remembers, "growing up in Boyle Heights I had a fight every day because I had a tie on. And I had more fights than the average kid!" His mother's main emphasis was on school. She made sure that he went to school, received good grades, and lived up to wearing a tie. Edward Roybal notes, "That influence has remained with me today. One of the reasons that I can get things done is because I prepare myself. As long as you are prepared you have a chance. When I go into a conference with the Senate, I study and do my homework carefully and do not go in unprepared."

When asked who influenced him (besides the jeweler) to achieve at such an early age, Edward Roybal replied: "My mother motivated me. She was a fighter. In junior high school I wanted to take college prep classes, but my adviser told me it was no use doing that because your people can't get these jobs anyway. So, instead, he put me into industrial arts courses, like electrical shop and wood shop. I went home and my mother asked, 'Do you want to be an electrician?' I said that I didn't. 'So, why are you taking those classes?' She put on her bonnet, went down to school, spoke to the principal and the adviser, and the result? I was put into the algebra class! That kind of spirit was the one motivating factor that made me believe that I was just as good as everybody else and to this day I still think so."

When Edward Roybal graduated from high school it was during the Depression years, a time when many people were without work. He took a six-month enlistment with the Civilian Conservation Corps (CCC), which was under the United States Army. The pay was $30 per month, and $25 of that went to his family. It helped them during those hard times without needing to accept public assistance. With the CCC, Roybal helped build roads, storm drains, and fight forest fires. The roads still exist today in Sequoia National Park in California, but the hardest job, Roybal remembers, was fighting forest fires. The longest forest fire that he was involved in took two weeks to contain. Whenever a CCC camp was assigned a job, they were graded and were in competition with other CCC camps for the top ranking. Their work and even the tents they lived in were inspected every day. "Everything we did was in fair competition with others, and excellence was always rewarded. It made it possible for us to compete and do the best we possibly could in all our endeavors." The reward was one or more extra days off, which meant they could go back home to spend a long weekend with their families.

The CCC gave honorable and dishonorable discharges from the camp. A dishonorable discharge meant that the person could not return for another enlistment. An honorable discharge for Edward Roybal resulted in being placed in charge of his platoon when he later served in the Army during World War II. He felt there were additional advantages as a CCC graduate:

"I was able to avoid many problems that a poverty-stricken kid would encounter if he remained in the Boyle Heights area. One young man who grew up with me did not go to CCC and ended up in prison with all kinds of problems. It wasn't just a matter of being poor that we were there. It was a matter of pride. We were there because we were poor, that's true, but we stayed because we were good."

Edward Roybal left the CCC to attend college. He studied business administration with an emphasis in accounting at the University of California, Los Angeles (UCLA), Southwestern College, and Kaiser College. His first job after graduating from college was with the cost accounting unit at 20th Century Fox Studios. His job was to sit on the set when a motion picture was being filmed and to time how long it took. Using that information, he would then determine what it cost for everything that took place on the set.

Working with 20th Century Fox eventually led him into health education. The Tuberculosis Association visited the movie studios to encourage employees to take a TB test. Tuberculosis is a contagious disease that mainly affects the lungs. At that time, testing had started in schools, but parents were not giving permission to test their children. The TB Association hoped that giving the test to parents at their places of business would help with understanding the need for testing and to increase permissions for testing their children. Roybal became interested and volunteered his help for two years. When an opportunity occurred to run one of the first mobile X-ray units, he was given a job. In addition, he became a public health educator and eventually one of the Directors of Health Education for the Los Angeles County Tuberculosis and Health Association.

As a Health Education Director, Edward Roybal attended many seminars at universities across the nation specializing in public health and community organizations. The challenge of his job was to get people to take TB tests and once the skin test showed positive, to have chest X-rays taken, and finally to receive treatment in a sanitarium. One of the difficulties that Roybal remembers was the problem with placing minority group patients into sanitariums because of racial discrimination. He started a campaign against the old system and was able to change it, but it was a struggle. Because TB can be easily spread, much like the common cold, Roybal talked (in Spanish) about this disease in a film which was shown before the main movie in Spanish language theaters around the country. Today, because of Roybal's ef-

Congressman
Edward R. Roybal

forts and those of others who educate the public about health, tuberculosis is not as common as it once was.

In the late 1940s, several people that Edward Roybal worked with encouraged him to run for political office. They knew him as a skilled organizer, hard worker, and excellent communicator. The first time he ran for office, he lost by less than four hundred votes. After a few years, Edward Roybal was elected to the Los Angeles City Council at the age of thirty-three. He was reelected for three additional terms, twice running unopposed.

In 1962, Roybal was elected Representative from California's 25th District to the United States House of Representatives in Washington, D.C. (The House of Representatives and the Senate make up the Congress, the legislative branch of our government.) The two most important areas in Edward Roybal's career as a congressman are health and education. He has reflected, "What I think is most important is what I have done in the fields of health and education. These are the things that have given me the most satisfaction."

Edward Roybal is personally responsible for establishing the ten nationwide gerontology centers and for taking steps toward a national health plan. The gerontology centers are dedicated to researching the medical problems of senior citizens to discover what the aging process is and how to increase our life-spans. Ten additional centers are scheduled to be completed by the year 2000. For several years, Congressman Roybal has led his committee in preparing a national health plan for this country. He has said, "We are the only industrialized nation that doesn't have a plan, besides South Africa." His committee has held hearings, done research, and authored legislation to write such a plan. Some parts have already been approved by Congress but, according to Roybal, "not enough."

Edward Roybal and family. Left to right: Edward, Jr., Lucille Roybal Allard, Congressman Roybal, Mrs. Lucille Roybal, Lillian.

In the realm of education, Roybal presented the first bilingual education bill. It was not adopted in full, but parts were incorporated into the current legislation. Through California State University, Los Angeles, and the neighboring gerontology center, students will be able to receive a special advanced degree in health and human services. It will be a two-year program with half the time spent taking university courses and the other half in on-the-job experience and training at the gerontology center and the Roybal Comprehensive Health Center. According to the congressman, this will prepare students to play an important role in the field of health dealing with senior citizens. Also through this program students will help in caring for the poor and will be encouraged to pursue their doctorate degrees.

Edward and Lucille Roybal have three children, Lucille, Lillian, and Edward, Jr. Their oldest daughter, Lucille Roybal Allard, has also become involved in a political career. She is representative of the 56th District (in Los Angeles) to the California State Assembly. When asked to describe her father, Assemblywoman Allard replied, "As a father he emphasized honesty and telling the truth. He said you always had to remember that whatever actions you took or decisions you made, you had to do it from the perspective, as he put it, that 'you had to be able to go to bed with yourself.' It didn't matter what anyone else thought because you had to feel good about what you did or didn't do."

Congressman Edward Roybal has felt satisfied with his many accomplishments for the community that he serves and for the nation. His main goal has always been to solve problems and to get things done. He is proud of his work in the health and education fields and has considerable respect for teachers and nurses. His reasons are: "Teachers because of the influence a good teacher can have on the minds of the children, and nurses for what they can do for humanity. Those are the two professions that I greatly admire. I would like to be remembered as an advocate of good nursing, good health, and good education."

Dan Sosa, Jr.

"Money does not make life. Now, as a public servant, I make half of what I made before as an attorney. Real success in life is knowing that you helped others to change their lives for the better." Dan Sosa, Jr., has helped many others to change for the better in his work as Senior Justice of the State Supreme Court of New Mexico.

Dan Sosa was born November 12, 1923, and reared in Las Cruces, New Mexico. At the age of four years, his parents divorced and his mother dedicated herself to rearing Dan and his sister, Lucy. His father remarried and spent the majority of his time with his new family. Being a single parent, Dan's mother worked hard to support her family, and finances were limited.

When Dan was about eight years old, he wanted

Dan Sosa and sister Lucy Sosa Magallanes, Las Cruces, New Mexico

to help out by selling newspapers and shining shoes. Justice Sosa recalls going down to the courthouse after school, where his uncle, the sheriff, had his office. At the time, he lived in his uncle and aunt's home with his mother and sister. He enjoyed visiting with his uncle at the office and giving him a complimentary shoeshine. On one occasion, voices coming from one of the courtrooms caught young Dan's attention and he quietly slipped in to watch. "I saw the D.A. [district attorney] presenting his case and was impressed with this brilliant advocate for the state," he remembers. "I thought then that I wanted to be a D.A. too."

Throughout his schooling, Dan Sosa studied hard and participated in sports. He played on the first Las Cruces High School basketball team to go all the way to the state championship and win. An athletic scholarship was awarded to Dan for New Mexico State A&M (now New Mexico State University). However, his college education was interrupted by the start of World War II.

"I remember very clearly what I was doing on December 7, the day Pearl Harbor was bombed. I was out hunting jack rabbits and my mother was home listening to the radio. When I came in, she told me about what she had just heard. I had just started school and I was doing poorly in engineering. So I took the exams to become a cadet and joined the U.S. Air Force." Dan Sosa served as a bombardier in B-24 Liberators. He flew thirty-five combat missions over enemy-occupied Europe, returning home as a commissioned officer and decorated veteran.

Dan Sosa took advantage of the G.I. Bill, which provided support for veterans to finish their schooling. In 1947, he graduated from New Mexico State A&M with a Bachelor of Science degree in business administration. His interest in sports continued as a member of the college basketball team, and as an elementary schoolteacher and basketball coach in one of his first jobs after graduating. He was successful in leading this team to a victorious regional championship.

After his first year of teaching, Dan Sosa came to a crossroads in his life. He remembered the fascination he had as a young boy with becoming a district attorney, and turned down another job opening that occurred. "The principal of the school that I worked for ran for superintendent of schools and won. He wanted me to take over the principal's position. I had other interests developing. My family was active politically. My uncle had been elected sheriff and I was the district chairman of the Young Democrats after the war."

Dan Sosa decided to enroll in the University of New Mexico School of Law. Every summer he worked for several state agencies in Santa Fe to help pay for his law education. It was during one of these summers that he met and married his wife, Rita Ortiz. In 1951, Dan Sosa received his Juris Doctorate degree. He began his law career by accepting a position as a special agent for the federal government. Next, he served as assistant district attorney and in 1952, he was elected city judge of Las Cruces, New Mexico.

In 1956, he felt that the time had come to move onward. Judge Sosa wanted to run for the position of district attorney, but this would not be a simple task. Justice Sosa recalls, "I was told that I could not run because I was Hispanic and this was an Anglo district. Also, it was ironic that the same towheaded lawyer who was my early role model supported the man who would be my opponent!"

Judge Sosa knew that this campaign would present a challenge and he felt very strongly that he would be able to do the best job. He still recalls the special way in which he helped voters to remember his name. "I clipped out a newspaper picture of me at the time when I returned home from the war. I walked the district and told people about what I did in World War II, showed them the newspaper picture, and some had already read the article. I gave a penny to each person that I met and talked with." The people did remember Dan Sosa and elected him to the position of district attorney by two hundred votes. When he ran again for a second four-year term, he won by four thousand votes.

Dan Sosa had represented many Hispanics as a lawyer in private practice and, as district attorney, he continued his interest in ensuring their civil rights. The filing of the first discrimination-in-hiring and discrimination-in-education cases in the state of New Mexico were coordinated by Dan Sosa. As one of the original group of attorneys, he also helped to create and establish the Mexican American Legal Defense and Educational Fund (MALDEF). He was elected to MALDEF's first board of directors and served until April, 1975.

During this period, Justice Sosa's accomplishments became known to the judicial selection committee of the New Mexico State Bar Association.

Portrait as Chief Justice of the Supreme Court of New Mexico

Also at this time, an opening needed to be filled on the State Supreme Court and Dan Sosa's name was recommended to the governor, Jerry Apodaca. On July 3, 1975, Dan Sosa was appointed by Governor Apodaca as Justice to the New Mexico State Supreme Court. In the following year, Justice Sosa was elected to a full eight-year term. He became Chief Justice in 1979 and two years later became Senior Justice. The Senior Justice is the person with the most years of continuous service and acts in the absence of the Chief Justice.

When asked about his schedule for a typical month, Senior Justice Sosa replied that he is involved with two main areas of responsibility: (1) reviewing judgments formally submitted to the State Supreme Court and (2) hearing emergency arguments about overruling a decision that a judge from a lower court has made. His remaining time is spent studying case information, such as testimony from witnesses and court records, meeting with justices to discuss cases, drafting opinions, and preparing for the final filing of the decision.

The State Supreme Court of New Mexico hears all cases (from all lower courts, including the Court of Appeals) that are formally submitted to it. Some state supreme courts hear only those cases that they feel are of important public policy. However, New Mexico's state constitution provides that all people should have access to this court. Everyone constitutionally in New Mexico has the right of appeal. At least three days out of each month are reserved to hear oral arguments from attorneys about these cases.

Every Wednesday is set aside to review special motions or petitions. Attorneys argue their cases before a panel of three Supreme Court justices unless it is a capital case. The justices discuss the case together, form an opinion, and file an official court order.

Senior Justice Sosa's reputation spread through the state, contributing to his successful reelection to

New Mexico Supreme Court Justices, 1987. Left to right: Justices William R. Federici, Mack Easley, Dan Sosa, Jr., J. Vern Payne, Edwin L. Felter.

a second eight-year term. His list of achievements continues to grow. He has received the Lex Award from the Mexican American Bar Association in Los Angeles and the Valerie Kantor Award for Extraordinary Achievement—honors given to an individual who has made outstanding contributions to the Hispanic community and the law. In 1987, the Conference of Chief Justices of all Latin-American countries, Spain, France, and the United States was held. Senior Justice Dan Sosa earned the distinction of being selected to represent the United States. Together, they discussed the role and responsibilities of judges around the world and ways to improve in their profession.

Even with his very busy schedule, Justice Sosa has always made time to do things with his family. In particular, every spring break he would gather the family together for a vacation to Mazatlán, a beach resort town on the western coast of Mexico. Justice Sosa has commented that he never told his own children to be lawyers. However, two of his seven children—the eldest, Dan, and Steven—have sought careers as attorneys. Three daughters, Rita Jo, Loretta, and Roberta, are residing in Las Cruces with their own families. The youngest son, Martin, and daughter Anna live in Santa Fe, New Mexico. Justice Sosa and his wife, Rita, have seventeen grandchildren altogether.

Throughout his career, Dan Sosa has felt strongly about issues involving racial discrimination. He has worked to change laws which limit personal rights or freedoms because of race. He has said, "Prejudice deprives the person discriminated against from reaching their full potential and deprives society from allowing this flower to bloom."

Equally important to Justice Sosa is the belief that individuals must also try their hardest to improve. When people think of Senior Justice Dan Sosa, he would want them to remember him as "a person who tried to be the best he could be."

Luis Valdez

"Whenever you run into an obstacle there is a creative way around it. It makes no sense to ram your head up against the wall and make yourself bloody. You can find another way—over the wall or around it or under it. Remember, your greatest strength and powers and treasures are within you, and you carry around all you need to deal with your own life."

This has been Luis Valdez's attitude about life throughout his childhood and as an adult. He is a writer, director, and actor. One of his most popular films that he wrote and directed is *La Bamba*.

Luis was born in Delano, California, on June 26, 1940. He was a second-generation American, the second of ten children born to Frank and Armida Valdez, who came to California from Arizona in the 1920s. During World War II, Luis' family worked their farm until the late 1940s when market prices fell and they lost the farm. The Valdez family then began to follow the migrant farm workers' path. Because migrant farm workers move from area to area, depending on the type of crop that is ready to harvest, it is necessary for children to change schools frequently and often the timing of the move is not the best. Luis Valdez recalls attending the first grade at a rural school near a farm labor camp. The harvest season was over, but his family could not move on because their truck had broken down.

"I would take my lunch to school every day in a paper sack, and I would save the sack to reuse it the next day. We couldn't afford lunch pails. One day I couldn't find my bag in the closet, and when I found it the teacher had soaked my bag in a large container of water. She told me she was going to make papier-mâché masks. I asked her what these masks were for and she said for a play. So the following week I tried out and got a role—one of the leading roles. It was about Christmas with monkeys in the jungle and I was one of the monkeys. I had a costume and I had a mask and I felt on top of the world. The irony of it all is that a week before the play was to be performed, at Christmas time, my father got the truck fixed and we moved away."

Missing out on the school play created what Luis Valdez describes as an unfillable gap. He wanted to be in a play, to put on plays, and to be in plays with his friends. At the age of seven, he started staging

Young Luis Valdez and his family, Santa Cruz, California, summer 1946. Left to right: mother Armida, baby sister Irma, sister Lupe, father Frank, Luis.

some theatricals with his friends. This led to the making of puppets and the creation of his own characters. Using a cardboard box for a stage in his grandfather's garage, Luis would give performances that reflected his imagination. When he was helping his family in the fields during weekends or summers, he would daydream about what he was going to make next or the kind of show he was going to put on. Luis later recalled that this gave him a real tie with himself that he has never lost.

During his teenage years, Luis Valdez developed his artistic interests, as well as interests in other areas. He increased his skills in math and science and enjoyed reading. One type of reading that Luis especially liked was fairy tales because they seemed to "address a dimension that gave him power in his own life." Another subject that he read eagerly about was ventriloquism. He taught himself how to talk without moving his lips and became a ventriloquist, using a Jerry Mahoney doll that he received through a friend.

Luis Valdez's ventriloquist act became known around the San Jose, California, area and when KNTV, the local television station, started, he was invited to come onto their Sunday Spanish language show. The year was 1956, and Luis was given five minutes on black-and-white, live television to perform his act, in both English and Spanish. It was exciting to have all the kids in his school see him on TV. Luis wrote all of his own scripts, which utilized

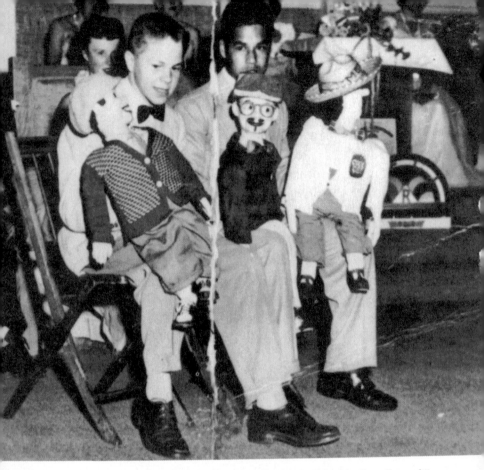

Luis Valdez (right) with "my best high school buddy, Ray Deutsch" performing as ventriloquists in San Jose in 1956. Ray and Luis were both sixteen years old.

dummies he had made, and included kids from the neighborhood. He was a huge success, held a regular spot every Sunday, and was paid five dollars a show.

It was amazing to Luis Valdez to get paid for something that he loved to do. "It would make me think about how long it would take at that time to make five bucks out in the fields, because that's what my family was really supporting itself on: farm labor. Doing television was a much brighter alternative than picking beans—or even strawberries, as much as I love to eat strawberries. That was a very important transition in my life. It certainly anchored me in the thought that I would like to go into show business."

When Luis graduated from high school he received a scholarship to San Jose State College and was a math and physics major. He thought he would end up in electronics like his older brother, who lives and works in "Silicon Valley" in California today. However, after a year of college, Luis wanted to return to his "most basic passion" and that was the theater. He became an English major and started writing plays. This led to an apprenticeship with his professors and the writing of his first serious one-act play. This play and the full-length play that he wrote and directed, *The Shrunken Head of Pancho Villa*, were big hits on campus.

At this time, Luis Valdez says, the elements in his life came together. His own experiences in the labor camps with the farm workers had never left him. When he was little, Luis remembers going to a movie house once with his brother Frank. In those days some of the theaters were segregated, but the boys did not know this, having just moved into a new town. The usher came and asked them to sit in the "Mexican section." Luis wanted to do something to help all minorities to achieve a certain level of human dignity, and at nineteen he joined a civil rights movement. All the social problems that were apparent to him while growing up came to a head and he became very political. But his interest in the theater had never left him either. His desire to do theater merged with his political ideals, and the idea of a farm workers' theater began to emerge.

While working with the San Francisco Mime Troupe during the mid-1960s, Valdez learned of Cesar Chavez and the United Farm Workers (UFW). When the UFW strike broke out, he went to Delano and started to organize a theater group which was to become the dynamic Teatro Campesino. He recalls having no resources: ". . . no money, no props, no scripts, no stage, no lights, no actors, nothing. All that was there was just the spirit of the people, but that was enough. People were willing to speak up and I had learned enough from my years in college and with the mime troupe to direct nonactors to improvise from their own experiences. What happened is that the Teatro Campesino took root and became a very vibrant element in the whole grape strike and, through its tours, in the whole Chicano community."

Luis Valdez and Teatro Campesino finished out the 1960s touring college campuses across the country. They were also invited to the Newport Folk Festival and performed with people like Joan Baez, Judy Collins, Bob Dylan, and Buffy Sainte-Marie.

A need for a permanent home brought the Teatro Campesino to San Juan Bautista, a small rural town surrounded by rolling California hills in its own little valley.

The quiet of San Juan Bautista allowed for the development of the Teatro's own acting techniques and materials. Throughout the 1970s, they produced many full-length plays, television programs, a few small films, and records that Mr. Valdez felt "still carried social content but tried to reach a larger and larger audience." The theater group toured western Europe six times, as well as many cities, large and small, in the United States. The performances took them from labor camps on flatbed trucks to the Senate courtyard in Washington, D.C., where their hosts were Robert and Edward Kennedy. Teatro Campesino was recognized as a professional theater group and received several grants following Luis Valdez's appointment to the California Arts Council by Governor Edmund G. Brown, Jr., in 1976.

During the late '70s, Luis Valdez was asked to write a play about the history of Los Angeles. The play he wrote is based on the Los Angeles "zoot suit riots" occurring around the early 1940s. Several Mexican-American youths were convicted on biased and unsubstantial evidence in the "Sleepy Lagoon" murder trial after the riots. Two of the central actors in this play were Edward James Olmos and Luis' brother Daniel Valdez. The actors wore zoot suits, described as "pants with wide legs and tight cuffs, a very long watch chain, a full-length coat, and a broad-brimmed hat with a flat top."

The award-winning *Zoot Suit* was a tremendous success in Los Angeles and went to New York. In 1978, Valdez was honored by being named to receive the Rockefeller Foundation Playwright-in-Residence Award for *Zoot Suit*. This play also launched Luis Valdez's career as a writer-director in motion pictures, after completing the film version of *Zoot Suit* for Universal Studios.

Luis Valdez then took the Teatro Campesino in another direction, which led to the creation of "Corridos" for television. *Corridos* are Mexican folk ballads and, in days past, also a form of stories that were relayed from town to town by singing "reporters." "Corridos" became a public television presentation featuring Linda Ronstadt singing and enacting the Mexican-American folk songs. Valdez went on to work on other films, and *La Bamba* was one that rose to great popularity and success. This movie was about Ritchie Valens, who spent much of his early years working in the California farm labor camps before becoming a rock 'n' roll idol of the 1950s. With Teatro, Valdez is continuing to work as a writer and director in the world of film, but he produces Christmas plays at the San Juan Bautista Mission as a yearly tradition.

Luis Valdez and his wife, Lupe, were both raised in California's San Joaquin Valley and are from large families. They met while Luis was teaching a class at Fresno State University. She was a student in the class and later joined Teatro Campesino. After a few years they married and now have three sons, whose names reflect a sense of their heritage and cultural background. Anahuac, born in 1971, wants to become an actor and has performed in a TV pilot for CBS. His name is Aztec, meaning "a place surrounded by water." Kinan, two years younger, is a graphic artist, a mathematician, and writer. His name is Mayan and means "solar energy." Lakin, "sunrise or another dawn," was born in 1978 on the very day that Luis Valdez finished writing the play, *Zoot Suit*. According to Luis Valdez, the very first words Lakin spoke were "zoot suit." The boys have grown up with the Teatro Campesino and have become a part of the new generation of members whose ages range from five to seventeen years old. Valdez has noted that the rich environment of the theatrical group has helped the children do well in school by developing their creativity and expression.

As an award-winning playwright, motion picture and television writer-director, Luis Valdez is an inspiring role model for the people of Teatro Campesino and for all Hispanics. He feels, however, that though he can give encouragement as a role model, first of all you must encourage yourself. When asked how he came to this understanding, he replied:

"There was something that happened to me in the third grade. We had a young teacher—I'm sure just out of college, now that I think of it, but at that time she seemed like a full-grown woman. She was the third-grade teacher and in the next class over was the sixth-grade teacher. He was also the shop teacher and he and the third-grade teacher were sweet on each other. In the sixth grade in shop, the teacher had this truck built by the students. It was all made out of wood with wooden wheels and painted bright yellow. The sixth-grade teacher gave it to the third-grade teacher and she brought it in to show to our class. She said that she was going to award this truck to the best-behaved boy in the class during the next month. Most of the boys were on their best behavior, and I certainly thought I was on my best behavior.

"The teacher had a pet that she always picked, an Anglo boy, a grower's son. She always picked him as a monitor to pass out papers. One of the students asked, on a separate occasion, why she always picked him. She told the class that he was the son of a grower and that his father employed many Mexican people and when we grew up, chances are we would be working for him. So it made a lot of sense for him to lead the group, since that was his destiny.

"After the month, the time came to award the truck and she gave it to the same boy. I had seen him goofing up in class, so I knew we were getting gypped. Now, I suppose I could have gotten choked up with a sense of rage and injustice and just not done anything after that. But what happened to me, as with the play incident in the first grade, is I felt

Luis Valdez, 1988

that if he was going to have that truck, let him have it. I'm going to make my own!

"I got working tools together and I put a truck together and it was terrible! It didn't look at all like the one that the sixth graders had made, but I kept working at it. I made another one and another one. For about three or four years running there, I got into making model cars and trucks with pieces of wood, and eventually these little trucks got better and better and better. My mother even put them on the mantle to show them off to relatives, and other friends would come along and want them.

"So what I discovered is that very often when something is taken from you, something is also being given to you. What was given to me was the capacity to make my own toys, the capacity to connect with my own sense of self-worth.

"I didn't have to accept the fact that I would end up working for that boy. I didn't have to accept the fact that I would never have a truck like that. I could make myself a truck like that.

"It's not a question of 'us' and 'them.' It's not you against the world. It's you and yourself. You can give yourself things that no one else can give you and that's what I try to tell kids today. Go for it!"

William Velasquez

 Michael Dukakis was running for president of the United States. Willie Velasquez had been selected to introduce the candidate at the Texas Democratic Convention at 10:00 A.M. on June 18, 1988. Instead, on that date and at that time, Mr. Dukakis attended Willie Velasquez's funeral, for he had died quite suddenly at the age of forty-four. Instead of Mr. Velasquez praising Governor Dukakis, it was Dukakis who praised the accomplishments of Velasquez, the man whose motto was *"Su Voto Es Su Voz,"* or "Your Vote Is Your Voice."

Willie Velasquez believed that people would not register or vote if their favorite candidates could not win. He worked for nearly twenty years to help people to register and vote, and to make sure that their candidates had a fair chance to win. To him, "real politics" meant that people were able to participate in the system and improve their own lives.

William C. Velasquez, known as Willie, was born on May 9, 1944, in Orlando, Florida, while his father was stationed there during World War II. Soon after Willie's birth, the family moved back to their home in San Antonio, Texas. Willie was raised in the Cenizo Park *barrio* located in the Edgewood district on the west side of the city. He was one of five children, and his father was a butcher for the Swift Meat Company.

Willie had a large extended family, with grandparents, aunts, uncles, and cousins all living near one another. During one period, there were five houses of relatives all within a block and a half of each other. Even when Willie's family moved to different houses, it was only six or seven houses away and always within just a few blocks.

Living close to several generations of relatives influenced Willie's life as a child and his ideas as an adult. Willie was most impressed by his grandfather, Fidel Cardenas, who was born in Mexico. Mr. Cardenas went to college and was very successful until the Depression of the 1930s, a time of severe economic hardship for many people. Willie vividly remembered his grandfather's stories about the heroes of Mexico and tales of the Mexican Revolution. Grandfather Cardenas taught Willie that ideals, reasons, and principles were important. Willie Velasquez commented that his grandfather never became

Four-year-old Willie Velasquez on a pony

a United States citizen, but he was very interested in politics and elections. Willie's uncles were also very political. Willie remembered that even when he was eight and nine years old, his parents would let him stay up, talking politics with his uncles until three o'clock in the morning. If the discussion took place at an uncle's home, he was even permitted to sleep there and go to school directly the next day.

Willie was taught that education was to be valued. As long as he could remember, his parents always said that he would be going to college, and he worked toward that goal. He began elementary school in the public system. By the third grade, however, his parents had saved enough money so that he could enter Holy Rosary, a private school. Willie sold newspaper subscriptions to help pay tuition at both Central Catholic High School and Saint Mary's University in San Antonio.

Willie listened to many discussions about both Mexico and politics as he grew up. He was interested in what he heard and decided that he wanted to be in the foreign service. During college, he was selected as an intern (a person being trained for a job) with the U.S. State Department in Washington, D.C. He was the only Mexican American out of about 140 interns at the time. Later, he began to change his focus from foreign service to civil rights. He graduated from Saint Mary's University and continued his studies in graduate school. During these years he became involved in the Chicano civil rights move-

ment. Willie Velasquez was only a few months from
earning his master's degree when he was recruited
to work for the United Farm Workers, the union
under Cesar Chavez.

Willie dropped out of graduate school and helped
farm workers to organize in the Rio Grande Valley
of Texas. He also worked as a boycott coordinator
to encourage the public not to buy certain produce
from farms that did not use unionized labor. The
pay was five dollars per week, but low pay was only
part of the sacrifice he made. The cause of the farm

*Willie Velasquez (seated, third from right), ten years old, with the
Holy Rosary School baseball team*

workers was controversial. He experienced much un-
pleasant reaction, both against the farm workers and
against people of Mexican descent. He has said that
"even to suggest that farm workers get decent salaries
was considered radical and subversive . . . that the
union would subvert the American public." His father, president of the local union at the meat packing
plant, understood. The rest of his family was also
supportive. Willie said that the strong reactions were
still "tough for a young person."

Willie Velasquez helped to create several Chicano
civil rights groups, both during and after his school
years. In the late 1960s, he met José Angel Gutierrez,
another Saint Mary's student in San Antonio. Along
with several others, they formed an organization
which wanted to unite Mexican Americans so they
could gain political power. Willie left the group,
however, as it formed into the political party, La
Raza Unida (The United Race). He did not think
that a separate third party was the way to involve
Mexican Americans in politics. He preferred organization at the community level, and formed a community action group in San Antonio in 1968. La
Raza Unida lasted for about ten years, but never
achieved the support it needed to elect state or national officials.

While organizing in San Antonio, Mr. Velasquez
began to realize how voter registration seemed to
be a key to political participation. In 1972, he decided to devote himself to voter registration. He

founded the Southwest Voter Registration Education Project. SVREP soon was involved in more than just registration, as it branched into conducting surveys and lawsuits.

People would not register or vote if they were not interested in the issues, so Willie ordered surveys to uncover which issues were important to the people. The results surprised him. He had assumed that most people believed the elections for president, governors, and senators were most important, but the poll said no. People were really more interested in local elections and issues. Discrimination and prejudice were not the most meaningful issues; poor drainage of sewer systems and street potholes in their neighborhoods were more important to most of the people. On the west side of San Antonio, streets were not properly paved. In Willie's old school district, Edgewood, about half the teachers did not even have the qualifications usually required to teach. Once the Mexican Americans were discussing such local issues that affected them, Willie knew that they were more likely to take a real and active interest in politics and voting. They had the chance to really control their own communities.

Voter registration and opinion surveys would help to include more Mexican Americans in politics. At the same time, though, unfair election systems prevented people from becoming interested or involved. SVREP began filing lawsuits against unfair election practices and systems. They were joined by other organizations, such as the Mexican American Legal Defense and Educational Fund (MALDEF) and the Texas Rural Legal Aid.

In Texas, where this early legal activity took place, there were many obstacles. "Gerrymandering"—creating oddly shaped voting districts—gave an unfair advantage to those in power who had drawn the districts. The "at-large" voting system meant that the majority population in a large area would probably be represented, but other people might not. Both of these practices diluted the voting power of certain groups of people. Sometimes ballots given to Mexican Americans were a different color. They were easy to spot and separate out. In some cases, Mexican Americans were discouraged from voting by a county clerk who questioned their right to vote, saying they did not live in the county when in fact they did. At times, a poll tax, or fee to vote, was charged.

In 1975, SVREP became even more effective when Mexican Americans and other minorities became protected under the Voting Rights Act of 1965. This act was originally passed to guard the rights of black voters in the South. Unfair practices which were now unlawful did not stop automatically, but they had to be challenged on an individual basis and then brought to court.

Mr. Velasquez said he always tried to be polite when gathering information to challenge a district. He knew people were often angry and resentful when they saw him, or one of his workers, coming to investigate. Most of the time, records are handed over without incident because they are public and anyone is entitled to see them. One of the staff members, however, recalled that he was once warned to get out of a certain town by sunset, in Old West fashion. That worker made sure to leave on time and there was no trouble.

Beginning in 1974, Willie Velasquez was executive director of Southwest Voter Registration Education Project, and in 1985 he became its president. Since its early days, the organization has greatly expanded. It has conducted over 1,000 registration drives in 200 cities in seven southwestern states, and Hispanics are the fastest growing group of registered voters. Of the eighty-six lawsuits it has filed, eighty-five have been won and the other one has been appealed, which means it is being reconsidered by the court. Between 1977 and 1987, the number of Hispanic officeholders in the country doubled, almost half of them in Texas where SVREP has worked the longest. Also, there has been a change in attitude. Many Mexican Americans now believe that their vote can make a difference and that their candidates can help them improve their lives.

Willie Velasquez summarized the efforts of SVREP: "Now it's real politics! Here in Texas with Southwest, I never really thought we would do so well. We are the fastest growing group in registration and elected officials. Now California is the weak point." California is the state with the largest number

Willie Velasquez addressing a student group, 1981

of Latinos who are eligible to register and vote, but it does not have the largest number of Latino voters. SVREP wants to change this. There is already a shift in efforts to California, and it remains the challenge for the future. SVREP has also helped Native Americans, Asian Americans, blacks, and other minorities to gain political power in the Southwest. There has been activity in a total of seven states: Texas, California, New Mexico, South Dakota, Colorado, Arizona, and Utah.

As the 1988 elections approached, Willie Velasquez was asked to describe his job at SVREP. He said, "Southwest Voter is private and receives no federal, state, or local government money. Therefore, one part of my job is to raise money." (In 1987, it had a budget of $1 million, with money coming from foundation grants, corporations, churches, labor unions, and individuals.) "I also make sure that Southwest Voter can undertake campaigns. I enter into decisions on lawsuits, oversee polling and surveying, and go on-site. At the peak, there were two hundred campaigns in one year and I organized between thirty and thirty-five of them. There is much travel!"

Willie Velasquez spent most of his daily time working as president at SVREP, but he was also involved in other activities as well. He taught at Harvard University for a term. He was often asked to give advice about the concerns of Mexican Americans to elected officials and candidates running for office. He was very interested in our country's policies in Central America and he took trips to the region. He wanted to form ties with leaders in Latin America to encourage free and fair elections, and he wanted Hispanic Americans to be involved in United States foreign policy in Latin America.

Willie Velasquez did not have much free time. When asked his favorite hobby, he answered,

Willie Velasquez, April, 1988

"Watching my boy play soccer!" Mr. Velasquez and his wife, Jane, had three children: Carmen Maria, Catarina Inez, and Guillermo. He said that all his children were affected by his work, and he spoke of "many stimulating discussions." He said that the children were so knowledgeable that even the youngest, Guillermo, once corrected him as they talked. He added, "They are all very up-to-date on politics. They play the 'Central America Game' and name all the countries and their capitals in one minute, twenty-two seconds. They know geography and know what's happening."

Mr. Velasquez wanted to make sure his children got good grades so that they could have a chance at their goals. He believed that children have a responsibility to study for a good future and schools have a responsibility to provide good education. He felt that SVREP had helped education by filing lawsuits which permitted the elections of new school board members. He thought that schools had improved since the time when he had been taught by some unqualified teachers.

Willie Velasquez knew SVREP was working. He was proud that more minorities registered, voted, and were elected. He worked hard for these goals and he followed a very busy schedule. Early in 1988, he began feeling tired and ill. An aide said that he thought his decline in health was the result of too much work. However, his doctors soon diagnosed a cancerous tumor in one of his kidneys. Before going to Houston for an operation, he found time for his favorite activity, watching Guillermo play in a soccer match. Surgery was performed, but just two weeks later, on June 15, 1988, Willie Velasquez died from the cancer.

Willie Velasquez devoted much of his life to involving more people in voting and politics. He wanted ordinary people to realize that they were important and could make a difference. SVREP will continue the work which was so important to him. He looked forward to a better future, especially for minorities. During an interview just two months before his death, he reviewed the recent progress of Mexican Americans. He thought back to the late 1960s, when he was still a student, and then he exclaimed, "After all that has happened, it has only been twenty years!"

Selected Bibliography

Personal or telephone interviews were made by the authors with subjects covered in the book or with their aides or assistants.

CESAR CHAVEZ

Daniel, Cletus. "Cesar Chavez and the Unionization of California Farm Workers" in *Labor Leaders in America*, edited by Melvin Dubovsky and Warren Tine. Urbana: University of Illinois Press, 1987.

Gaines, Judith. "Cesar Chavez & The United Farm Workers." *Nuestro*, November, 1985.

Levy, Jacques. *Cesar Chavez, Autobiography of La Causa.* New York: W. W. Norton & Company, 1975.

Shagan, Louis. "After 36 Days, Chavez Halts Protest Fast." *Los Angeles Times*, August 22, 1988.

Yinger, Winthrop. *Cesar Chavez: The Rhetoric of Nonviolence.* Hicksville, New York: Exposition Press, 1975.

HENRY CISNEROS

Applebome, Peter. "For San Antonio and Its Mayor, an Emergence Is Envisioned." *The New York Times*, February 22, 1988.

Cisneros, Hon. Henry G. "The American City." *Hispanic Business Monthly*, May, 1982.

Diehl, Kemper and Jarboe, Jan. *Cisneros, Portrait of a New American*. San Antonio: Corona Publishing Company, 1985.

Garcia, Ignacio. "San Antonio's New Mayor." *Hispanic Business Monthly*, May, 1982.

Lehman, Nicholas. "First Hispanic." *Esquire*, December, 1984.

PATRICK FLORES

Davidson, John. "A Simple Man." *Texas Monthly*, July, 1981.

Gann, L. H. and Duignan, Peter J. "Latinos and the Catholic Church in America." *Nuestro*, May, 1987.

McMurtrey, Martin. *Mariachi Bishop: The Life Story of Patrick Flores*. San Antonio: Corona Publishing Company, 1985.

Sandoval, Moises. "Archbishop Flores: Minister to His People." *Modern Ministries*, March, 1982.

"200 Faces for the Future." *Time*, July 15, 1974.

DOLORES HUERTA

Coburn, Judith. "Dolores Huerta: La Pasionaria of the Farmworkers." *Ms.*, November, 1976.

Huerta, Dolores. "Dolores Huerta Talks About Republicans, Cesar, Children, and Her Home Town." *La Voz del Pueblo*, November–December, 1972, in Servin, Manuel P., *An Awakened Minority: The Mexican Americans*. New York: Macmillan, 1974.

Huerta, Dolores. "Reflections on the UFW Experience." *The Center Magazine*, July–August, 1985.

NANCY LOPEZ
Hispanic Notables in the United States of America. Albuquerque: José Andres Chacon, publisher. Saguaro Publications, Inc., 1978.
"Nancy Lopez." *Current Biography*, September, 1978.
Newman, Bruce. "The Very Model of a Modern Marriage." *Sports Illustrated*, August 4, 1986.

VILMA MARTINEZ
Hernandez, Al Carlos. "Vilma Martinez, Una Chicana Ejemplar." *Nuestro*, September, 1981.
Johnson, Dean. "Chair of the Board." *Nuestro*, September, 1985.
Loper, Mary Lou. "Motherhood for Two Career Women." *Los Angeles Times*, May 13, 1984.
O'Connor, Karen and Epstein, Lee. "A Legal Voice for the Chicano Community: The Activities of the Mexican American Legal Defense and Educational Fund 1968–82" in De La Garza, R. O., et. al., eds., *The Mexican American Experience*. Austin: University of Texas Press, 1985.

LUIS NOGALES
Diaz, Tom. "Man on Top of a Roller Coaster." *Hispanic Review of Business*, October, 1984.
Jones, Alex. "A Reprieve for UPI." *The New York Times*, March 13, 1985.
Paull-Borja, Laura. "First Chicano Trustee Still Working for a Change." *Stanford Campus Report*, June 1, 1988.

EDWARD JAMES OLMOS
Breiter, Toni. "Edward James Olmos." *Nuestro*, May, 1983.

Denby, David. "Welcome to East L.A." *New York* magazine, April 18, 1988.

Garcia, Guy D. and reported by Dutka, Elaine. "Burning with Passion." *Time*, July 11, 1988.

Hamill, Pete. "Soul on Vice." *New York* magazine, September 29, 1986.

KATHERINE DAVALOS ORTEGA

"Biographical Sketch of The Honorable Katherine Davalos Ortega." Washington, D.C.: Department of the Treasury.

Curry, Bill. "Keynoter Ortega to Set Convention Tone." *Los Angeles Times*, August 20, 1984.

Fink, Mitchell, interviewer. "Katherine Ortega's Autograph Is One You Can Treasure." *Los Angeles Herald Examiner*, February 20, 1984.

"She Dwells in Possibility." *New Accountant*, October, 1986.

BLANDINA CARDENAS RAMIREZ

Congress and the Nation, Vol. VI, 1981–84. Washington, D.C.: Congressional Quarterly, 1985.

Los Angeles Times, May 16, 1987.

Ramirez, Blandina Cardenas. Videotaped interview by Marina Pincus, December, 1987. Partially broadcast on the television program "Heritage" on Public Television KLRN, San Antonio.

EDWARD R. ROYBAL

Hispanic Notables in the United States of America. Albuquerque: José Andres Chacon, publisher. Saguaro Publications, Inc., 1978.

"The Honorable Edward R. Roybal." Biographical sketch. 25th District, California.

DAN SOSA, JR.
Hough, Marie T., ed. in *The American Bench 1987/88*. Sacramento: Reginald Bishop Forster and Associates, Inc., 1987.
"Biographical Sketch of Dan Sosa, Jr." Santa Fe, New Mexico: Office of the New Mexico Supreme Court.

LUIS VALDEZ
Beale, Steve. "Connecting with the American Experience: An Interview with Luis Valdez." *Hispanic Business*, July, 1987.
Bixler-Valadez, Kathy L. and Valdez, Lucia I. "Luis Valdez—From Flatbed to Broadway." *Caminos*, September, 1980.
Diaz, Katherine A. "Luis Valdez: The Making of *Zoot Suit*." *Caminos*, September, 1981.
Lubenow, Gerald C. "Putting the Border Onstage." *Newsweek*, May 4, 1987.

WILLIAM VELASQUEZ
Kase, Kathryn and Pearson, Michael. "He Changed the World." *San Antonio Light*, June 19, 1988.
Posner, Michael. "A Surge in Hispanic Power." *Macleans*, May 14, 1984.
Vasquez, Juan. "Watch Out for Willie Velasquez." *Nuestro*, March, 1979.

Index

Achievement Council, The, 71
Advisory Board on Ambassa-
    dorial Appointments, 71
Advisory Committee on Small
    and Minority Business
    Ownership, 101
AFL-CIO, 9, 47
All-Time Career Money list,
    (golf), 57
Allard, Lucille Roybal, 128
Anheuser-Busch Companies, 71
Apodaca, Jerry, 135
Associated Press, 59, 83
Aztecs, *x, xi*
Aztlán, *xi*

Ballad of Gregorio Cortez, The,
    93–94
Bank of California, 87
Barrios, 5, 154
Berg, Patty, 52
Bilingual education, 70, 112, 127
Blake, Robert, 1

Braceros, 7, 10, 43, 44, 46
Brown, Edmund, G. Jr. (Jerry),
    71, 147
Bureau of Engraving and Print-
    ing, 101–102
Byrne, Christopher, Bishop, 31

California Arts Council, 147
California Commission on Post
    Secondary Education, 82
California State University, 91,
    127
Cardenas, Amelia, 106, 107, 118
Cardenas, Fidel, 154
Cardenas, José A., 111
Cardenas, Rudolfo, 107, 111,
    118
Carranza, Venustiano, 15
Carter, Jimmy, President, 71,
    112, 114
Castillo, Lieut. Martin, 88, 95–
    96
Castro, Fidel, 27

Chavez, Cesar, 1–13, 33, 45, 46
146, 157
children of, 6, 13
Chavez, Cesario, 2
Chavez, Dorotea, 2
Chavez, Fernando, 6, 13
Chavez, Helen Fabela, 4, 6, 10, 45
Chavez, Juana Estrada, 2, 4
Chavez, Librado, 2, 3
Chavez, Manuel, 6
Chavez, Richard, 48
Chavez, Vicky, 3
Chicano civil rights movement, 79–80, 111, 156, 158
Cisneros, Elvira Munguia, 15, 16, 21
Cisneros, George, 15, 16, 17, 21
Cisneros, Henry, 14–26, 70, 117
children of, 21, 25, 26
Cisneros, Mary Alice Perez, 20, 21
Civil rights, 68–70, 111, 114–116, 134, 156
Civilian Conservation Corps (CCC), 122–123
Columbia University, 67
Commemorative coins, 103
Commission on Civil Rights, Texas, 35
United States, 106, 114–116
Committee on Aging, 120
Communities Organized for Public Service (COPS), 22, 35
Community Service Organization (CSO), 5, 44, 45
Conference of Chief Justices, 138
Copyright Royalty Tribunal, 101
"Corridos" (television program), 148
Cortez, Gregorio, 88, 93–94

Cortez, Hernan, *x*
Crystal City, Texas, 111
Cursillo religious movement, 33
Curtis Cup team, 56

Delano, California, 4, 9, 13, 45, 146
Department of Health, Education, and Welfare, 20, 112
Depression, Great, *xii*, 2, 3, 122, 154
Díaz, Porfirio, 15
Dukakis, Michael, 153

East Los Angeles Junior College, 91
Eastern New Mexico University, 99, 104, 105
Edgewood Independent School District (San Antonio), 111, 154, 159
Education of a Woman Golfer, The, 60
El Pachuco, 88, 92–93
Election systems, 22, 70, 159, 160
Escalante, Jaime, 88, 96

Flores, Patricio, 28
Flores, Patrick F., Archbishop, 27–38
Flores, Trinidad, 28
Ford Foundation, 21, 68
Fresno State University, 149
Furey, Francis, Archbishop, 33, 35–37

Gandhi, Mahatma, 6
George Washington University, 20, 21
Gerontology centers, 126–128

Gerrymandering, 160
Girl Scouts, 41, 54
Golden Globe Award, 96
Golden West Broadcasters, 82
Grape boycott, 7, 8, 9, 33, 47
Gutierrez, José Angel, 158

Harvard University, 163
Head Start, 112
Health and Education Subcom-
  mittee, 120
Huerta, Dolores, 6, 39–49
  children of, 45–49
Huerta, Ventura, 45, 48

Jackson, Jesse, 1
John Paul II, Pope, 37–38

Kaiser College, 123
Keel, Howard, 92
Kennedy, Edward, 147
Kennedy, Ethel, 1
Kennedy, Robert, 1, 9, 11, 147
King, Martin Luther, Jr., 6
Knight, Ray, 58, 60
KNTV (television station), 143

La Bamba, 140, 148
Ladies Professional Golf Associ-
  ation (LPGA) 51, 52, 57,
  60
  Hall of Fame, 51–52, 62
La Paz (UFW headquarters), 9,
  10, 48
La Raza Unida, 158
Leal, Luis, Dr., *ix–xiii*
Lopez, Delma, 52, 56
Lopez, Domingo, 52
Lopez, Marina, 52
Lopez, Nancy, 51–62
  children of, 58, 60

Los Angeles City Council, 119,
  126
Los Angeles Community Redevelopment Agency, 82
Los PADRES, 35

MacArthur, Douglas, General,
  26
Martinez, James, 73
Martinez, Salvador, 64
Martinez, Vilma, 63–74
  children of, 71, 73, 74
Massachusetts Institute of Tech-
  nology (MIT), 21
Mayans, *x*
McDonnell, Donald, Father, 5
MECHA, 80
Melton, Tim, 57
Mexican-American Cultural
  Center (MACC), 35
Mexican American Legal De-
  fense and Educational
  Fund (MALDEF), 63, 68–
  70, 73, 74, 82, 115, 117,
  134, 160
Mexican Revolution, *xi, xii,* 15,
  88, 107, 154
Mexico, *x–xii,* 14, 15
  ancient empires, *x*
  migration from, *xi, xii,* 2, 14,
  15, 88–89, 107
Mexico-U.S. Policy Study Pro-
  gram, 117
"Miami Vice," 95–96
Mondale, Walter, 25, 112, 113
Munguia, Carolina Malapica, 15
Munguia, Romulo, 14, 15, 16
Munguia, Ruben, 15, 21

*Nancy Lopez's The Complete
  Golfer,* 60

National Association for the
Advancement of Colored
People (NAACP), 67, 115
National Bi-Partisan Commission
on Central America, 24
National Farm Workers Associ-
ation (NFWA), 5–7, 9,
45–47
National health plan, 126
National Hispanic Agenda, 25
National Hispanic Scholarship
Fund (NHSF), 35
National League of Cities, 20, 25
New Mexico State A&M, 132
New York State Division of
Human Rights, 68
Nixon, Richard, President, 81
Nogales, Alejandro, 76–78, 80,
87
Nogales, Florencia, 75–76, 78,
87
Nogales, Luis, 75–87
children of, 86–87
Notre Dame University, 25

Office of Catholic Services for
Immigrants, 35
Olmos, Edward James, 1, 88–
97, 147
children of, 92, 97
Olmos, Eleanor Huizar, 88–89
Olmos, Esperanza, 89
Olmos, Kaija Keel, 92, 97
Olmos, Pedro, 88–89, 91
Olmos, Peter, 89
Olsen, Ethel Ortega, 99–100
Ortega, Catarina Davalos, 98
Ortega, Donaciano, 98
Ortega, Katherine Davalos, 98–
105
Oscar Award nomination, 96

Otero Savings and Loan Association, 99, 100
Our Lady of the Lake University, 117

Perales, Alonso, 66

Ramirez, Blandina Cardenas,
106–118
son of, 118
Reagan, Ronald, President, 24,
98, 101, 104, 106, 114, 115
Regan, Donald, R., 101, 104
Republican National Conven-
tion, 104
Richardson, Elliot, 20
Ronstadt, Linda, 148
Ross, Fred, 5, 44
Roybal, Baudilio, 120
Roybal, Edward, 119–129
children of, 128
Roybal, Eloisa Tafoya, 120
Roybal, Lucille, 128
Roybal Comprehensive Health
Center, 128

St. Mary's Seminary, 32
Saint Mary's University, 156,
158
San Antonio, Texas, 14, 15,
19–23, 27, 35–38, 64, 68,
111, 154, 159
San Diego State University, 79
San Jose State College, 145
Santa Ana State Bank, 100
Sarasota Classic (golf), 51
Scripps, Edward, 83
Sea World of Texas, 23
Sheen, Martin, 1
*Shrunken Head of Pancho Villa,
The,* 145

Singer, Stuart, 67, 71
"Sleepy Lagoon" murder trial,
  93, 147
Sosa, Dan, Jr., 130–139
  children of, 138
  parents, 130
Sosa, Lucy, 130
Sosa, Rita Ortiz, 133, 138
Southwest Voter Registration
  Education Project
  (SVREP), 71, 159–163,
  165, 166
Southwestern College, 123
Spanish exploration, *x, xi*
Stand and Deliver, 96
Stanford University, 75, 79–81, 87
State Supreme Court of New
  Mexico, 130, 135–136
Sweetwater Country Club, 62

Target '90 (San Antonio), 23, 117
Teatro Campesino, 47, 146–
  149
Tenochtitlán (Mexico City), *x*
Texas A&M University, 19, 25
Texas Rural Legal Aid, 160
Treasurer of the United States,
  98, 101, 102, 103
Treaty of Guadalupe Hidalgo, *x*
Tuberculosis Association, 123–
  125
20th Century Fox Studios, 123

United Farm Workers, (UFW),
  1, 9, 10, 11, 13, 27, 47–
  49, 146, 157
United Press International, 75,
  81, 83–84
U.S. House of Representatives,
  48, 116, 120, 126
U.S.-Mexican War, *x*

U.S. Mint, 102–103
U.S. Savings Bond Division, 103
U.S. Senate, 116, 121
U.S. State Department, 156
University of California, 63, 71,
  82, 123
University of Massachusetts, 112
University of New Mexico, 133
University of Texas, 21, 66, 67, 110
University of Tulsa, 56
Univision, 75–76, 84

Valdez, Armida, 140
Valdez, Daniel, 147
Valdez, Frank, 140
Valdez, Luis, 47, 92, 140–152
  children of, 149
Valdez, Lupe, 148–149
Valens, Ritchie, 148
Vare Trophy, 57
Velasquez, Jane, 165
Velasquez, William, C. (Willie),
  71, 153–166
  children of, 165, 166
Vermeersch, Mary Benetia, Sis-
  ter, 31, 37
Voter registration, 5, 44, 158–
  163
Voting Rights Act of 1965, 160

Whitworth, Kathy, 52
White House Fellows, 20, 75, 81
Woman Athlete of the Year, 59
World War II, 4, 15, 26, 123,
  132, 134, 140

YOY Productions, 97
Young, Bob, 97
Young Democrats, 133

Zoot Suit, 92–93, 147–149